T0341460

Sales
Promotion

David Horchover

- ■ Fast track route to mastering all aspects of sales promotion

- ■ Covers all the key techniques for successful sales promotion, from understanding your customers to budget setting, and from promotional law to managing international promotions

- ■ Examples and lessons from some of the world's most successful businesses, including Autobytel.com, and Pepsi

- ■ Includes a glossary of key concepts and a comprehensive resources guide

≫EXPRESS EXEC.COM≪
essential management thinking at your fingertips

Sales Promotion

DAVID HORCHOVER

First published 2002 by
Capstone Publishing (a Wiley company)
8 Newtec Place
Magdalen Road
Oxford OX4 1RE
United Kingdom
http://www.capstoneideas.com

CIP catalogue records for this book are available from the British Library and the US Library of Congress

ISBN 1-84112-196-7

This book is printed on acid-free paper

Substantial discounts on bulk quantities of Capstone books are available to corporations, professional associations and other organizations. Please contact Capstone for more details on +44 (0)1865 798 623 or (fax) +44 (0)1865 240 941 or (e-mail) info@wiley-capstone.co.uk

Contents

Introduction to ExpressExec

ExpressExec is 3 million words of the latest management thinking compiled into 10 modules. Each module contains 10 individual titles forming a comprehensive resource of current business practice written by leading practitioners in their field. From brand management to balanced scorecard, ExpressExec enables you to grasp the key concepts behind each subject and implement the theory immediately. Each of the 100 titles is available in print and electronic formats.

Through the ExpressExec.com Website you will discover that you can access the complete resource in a number of ways:

» printed books or e-books;
» e-content – PDF or XML (for licensed syndication) adding value to an intranet or Internet site;
» a corporate e-learning/knowledge management solution providing a cost-effective platform for developing skills and sharing knowledge within an organization;
» bespoke delivery – tailored solutions to solve your need.

Why not visit www.expressexec.com and register for free key management briefings, a monthly newsletter and interactive skills checklists. Share your ideas about ExpressExec and your thoughts about business today.

Please contact elound@wiley-capstone.co.uk for more information.

Introduction: The Importance of Sales Promotion

» The importance and growth of sales promotion in today's markets.
» The participation by shoppers and buyers in sales promotion schemes.
» The amount spent on sales promotion, and comparisons with other activities.

If anyone doubts the importance or prevalence of sales promotion today, they need only pop to their local supermarket or pub, take a look in a national or local newspaper, or open the direct mail sent to their home or business address and they will instantly be given irrefutable proof of the volume and diversity of sales promotion activity in today's markets.

An American marketing academic, Philip Kotler, estimated that even as short a time ago as 10 years the ratio of advertising expenditure to sales promotion spending was roughly 60:40.[1] By 1997, the ratio had altered dramatically. Now, sales promotion is spending something in the region of 65–70% of the total. In real terms, sales promotion expenditure has been growing rapidly over the past 20 years.

More proof of the importance of the function and versatility of sales promotion is forthcoming in the oft-quoted Harris International Marketing *Marketing Week* survey, which showed that well over 70% of the population had participated in competitions or games relating to products or services.[2] Over a third had done so within the last month, over 40% had sent off a packet top or token for a free gift within the last four weeks, and an amazing 54% had used a money-off coupon. Although this survey is dated 1986, there is little reason to suggest that participation in any form of sales promotion has in any way diminished, even though the style or some of the techniques employed today may have different emphases placed upon them. Indeed, if the above figures are taken together, then as many as 60% of the population actively participate in some form of promotional activity in any one month. This makes sales promotion one of the biggest leisure activities or pastimes in the UK today. Here are some comparisons with other hobbies or activities:

» cycling (10%)
» swimming (13%)
» bingo (9%)
» pool or snooker (12%).[3]

To put sales promotion into even sharper focus as to its importance, it is as extensive as visiting a pub once a month or more. From these comparisons, one can therefore gauge the size and extent of promotional activity. But what does it all add up to in terms of money budgeted and spent?

It is almost impossible to put a figure on the exact amount that businesses and other organizations spend because the task falls down when deciding on definitions of sales promotion and ways of measuring the physical amounts. It is a relatively simple matter to discover how much has been spent on television and press advertising (in 1997, £3.1bn and £3.5bn respectively) and it is feasible to get a fair estimate of spending on direct mail (£1.1bn). Sports sponsorship accounted for a modest £300mn in 1999, and coming up fast is telemarketing with £110mn. Sales promotion, however, does not lend itself to any easy way of estimating its annual expenditure, as it extends to such a wide variety of activities. For years, the accepted total was "agreed" by the Advertising Association and the Institute of Sales Promotion to be approximately £7bn, but this has been revised upwards to around £10bn.[4] Even the European Promotional Marketing Association has tried to come up with a clearer picture, but the old problem still crops up – categorization. Many promotions use advertising, direct mail, telesales literature, price cuts (lost income or promotion cost?), or other media. And what about pack alterations to accommodate special deals? Whose budget do these come under?

Once these points have been taken on board and understood, it becomes apparent that sales promotion is not one of the also-rans in terms of the business or the overall marketing program but one of the most important planks in the structure of each. As has already been shown, it is also one of the most pervasive aspects of all our lives. And it will remain so. The pace of change is accelerating in most areas of our lives. We have only to look back even a few years to see what has happened with regard to the electronic media, the opening up of new markets with new or vastly improved products, and the increasing availability of services to wider audiences who can be reached more rapidly than ever. More people with more disposable income and aspirations to match will mean more, not less, promotional activity in the future, as companies vie with each other to ensure that they get more than their fair share of that disposable expenditure.

This means that every organization, whether trading for profit or "not for profit," will need to study, understand, create, and implement sales promotion in all its multifarious facets if they are to stay around, let alone succeed, in such a tough business environment. What follows is a route map or guide to help those unfamiliar with the sales promotion terrain to devise the right type of promotional activity and get the biggest bang from the drum for minimal effort (or make £1 sound like £100!).

NOTES

1 Kotler, P. (1967) *Marketing Management: Analysis, planning and control*, 9th ed. Prentice Hall, Englewood Cliffs, NJ.
2 *Marketing Week*, February 20, 1987.
3 Advertising Association (1997) *Marketing pocket book*. NTC Publications, Henley-on-Thames.
4 *The Times*, March 2, 2001.

Definition of Terms: What is Sales Promotion?

» The basis of business and marketing.
» The major elements of products and services – function, economics, psychology.
» The marketing mix and the four Ps – product, price, place, promotion.
» The main communication tools – advertising, sales promotion, publicity, direct selling, direct marketing.
» The impact of sales promotion on organizations.
» Definitions of sales promotion.

In order for a definition of sales promotion to be useful and meaningful, it is necessary to go back to the fundamentals of business and understand just what it is that organizations of any type need to know about their customers and prospects, as well as what systems they have of anticipating and satisfying their customers' needs.

Before marketing was "invented" this was usually the province of the entrepreneur, whose own feel for their business, together with the insight and flair that they had for moving the business forward, was usually the only system available. Today, this gut feeling is no longer good enough, although it might work for some for a short while. Now, businesses see customers and prospects as everyone's concern and they share the responsibility for thinking about customers' needs among all line managers. The marketing department might be the final home for the end result, but the executives who staff it today are really no more than first among equals when it comes to "keeping customers happy."

When it comes to providing products or services, the end result is a group of characteristics that can be be broken down into three basic elements:

1 function (i.e. what the product or service does);
2 economics (i.e. the cost of the product or service); and
3 psychology (i.e. the image of the product or service).

Most people would more readily understand these three elements as being the embodiment of a brand, with an inherent quality, value, and image that are either offered to, or created by, the user. It is the relationship which the company hopes to foster with its market, based on these three factors, that will determine how well it meets the needs of its targeted markets and creates that all-important competitive advantage over its rivals. This means that both the attitudes and behavior of a company's customers need to be appreciated, because sales promotion is, above all, about behavior.

Behavior means encouraging people to go out and buy a product or service and try it, for only by this method can the attitude of the buyer/user be formed or changed. Eventually, it is hoped that such trialists will become loyal users or customers and develop a long-term relationship. A good example of this is in the motor trade, where drivers of a certain make of car would never dream of changing their allegiance from one make to another, no matter what inducements were on offer, because they are not only satisfied with the product (function) and the price (economics), but they are also delighted with the image (psychology) of their car.

This brings us on to the core parts of marketing which, when listed, may seem mundanely obvious. Nevertheless, if one is to arrive at a proper definition of sales promotion, these have to be discussed, otherwise it is like trying to do advanced mathematics without being able to carry out multiplication, division, etc. The sum of these core parts forms what is known as the marketing mix.

THE MARKETING MIX

There is a relatively easy way to remember the four cornerstones of marketing, as they all begin with *P*.

1 *P* for *product* (or service): there has to be something offered for sale.
2 *P* for *price*: there has to be a price at which you can profitably sell something and which customers find fair value.
3 *P* for *place*: where are customers going to be able to purchase your product or service?
4 *P* for *promotion* and *presentation*.

(Note: Some marketing purists will introduce a fifth *P*, for *people*, as without people we have no business, and we do need to know about the people who currently buy, or could be induced to buy, our products and services.)

The role of sales promotion can now be seen as one of communication, even though it is just one of several methods by which a company attempts to alter or influence the behavior of its target market in the immediate short term. Here is a list of the main communication tools available to companies for this purpose. What is important to understand is that only very rarely can any element be employed in isolation for, as will be explained, each is basically interdependent.

» Advertising: this needs no further explanation, but it is all "paid-for" communication.
» Sales promotion: most people would quickly say that this consists of no more than incentives/inducements and various offers to

encourage people to behave in a certain manner. But this is not the true definition of sales promotion.

» Publicity: as opposed to paid-for communication, publicity is nothing more than information and, hopefully, good opinions carried by other parties.

» Direct selling: this is the personal approach, where seller and buyer/user actually meet face to face to conduct negotiations.

» Direct marketing: most people would readily identify direct mail (however it arrives) as being the main thrust of direct marketing, but it does also include any remote presentation to customers who can respond in the manner laid out by the promoting company.

The benefit of understanding these five tools is that one has a useful guide as to what each component can contribute to the overall marketing mix – companies can deduce which component will be the most appropriate to major in and how they should be combined to the optimum effect.

Here is a simple example of the far-reaching effects of a sales promotion scheme, which further demonstrates just how difficult it can be to separate the various strands of what makes a successful promotion and, therefore, to come up with a sensible definition. The key point is that a sales promotion can affect every aspect of the marketing mix. It can alter the packaging if, for example, the contents are increased by "33% extra free," or the pack contains a coupon or has a special flash price printed on it. Indeed, it may be decided to distribute the product well away from its normal sales locations for a special event, or to alter the theme of the advertising to accommodate the promotion. You could be talking about a promotion for a canned or bottled beer.

The thinking that lies behind more progressive practitioners in sales promotion is that a promotion has to be communicated to its intended audience by using one or more of the tools listed above. Rarely, however, will you see a piece of direct mail that does not include some further incentive to encourage replies, indeed early replies, as those who do respond early or quickly may well be entitled to some form of extra benefit denied to late participants. Companies will also advertise their promotions through the media to give as wide a coverage as possible and to merchandise their promotion. Whichever tool is used – advertising, direct selling, etc. – there is no diminishing the fact that a promotion is being communicated.

Sales promotion can, accordingly, be seen to be more than just one part of the communication mix. It is now seen to be the driving force that helps make short-term changes to the whole of the marketing mix, in order to bring about a change in behavior – now. Sales promotion is a frighteningly exciting ride to success or oblivion. The risks are high, but so are the rewards if you can get it right. And that is why it pays to know about the proper uses of sales promotion and how to create promotions that work.

DEFINING SALES PROMOTION

There are a great many attempted definitions of sales promotion, and as many arguments about it. These usually revolve around whether theme (brand-building) support and direct marketing activity are to be included within the discipline, and whether promotions can be long-term events. The Institute of Sales Promotion (ISP) has a fairly concise definition:

> "Sales Promotion comprises a range of tactical marketing techniques within a strategic marketing framework to add value to a product or service in order to achieve specific sales and marketing objectives."

A briefer version could well read:

> "The practice of offering temporary additional value to a brand in order to reach specific marketing objectives."

A number of useful points emerge from these two definitions.

» *Temporary*: how long is *temporary*? Once a promotion becomes ongoing, e.g. "every day low prices," it becomes part of the brand property or normal trading conditions and the whole point or purpose of such a promotion becomes lost within day-to-day trading.
» *Additional*: this will come over as:

» money (in the shape of reduced price, extra value, or a free sample)
» goods (either a branded item gift or competition)
» intangible benefits (for example charity or personality associations).

» *Specific marketing objectives*: if you can identify the objectives clearly, then you can devise the most effective solution.

The end result should be satisfied customer needs, all too frequently overlooked by those working at the coalface.

The Evolution of Sales Promotion

- » The early industrial era – production was king.
- » Brand proliferation.
- » Market segmentation – mass to almost individual.
- » The ''new'' marketing philosophy – the customer is king and quality matters.
- » The power of retailers over manufacturers.
- » Manufacturers and sales promotion.
- » Tactics and strategy.
- » Tighter control by management over sales promotion schemes.

Sales promotion has sometimes been labelled the world's second oldest profession! After all, if there is a product or, in this case, a service to be sold then it is a very rare one that does not require some form of promotion. Forget the Emerson story about building a better mousetrap and everyone will beat a pathway to your door! No self-respecting mousetrap-maker today would dare just sit back and wait for customers.

We have no historical records of sales promotional activity from times long past, but we can be assured that there were various devices, schemes, and methods used in keeping with the times which were employed to do the jobs that we expect modern-day promotions to fulfil. Back in the early industrial era, when factories churned out vast new ranges of ready-made goods and people bought them with a voracious appetite, there was probably little need for factory owners and producers to engage in any marketing practices, let alone much sales promotion, as they could usually shift all that could be made. Perhaps the only form of "promotion" about was the terms on which buyers/retailers bought, usually a discount for quick payment or settlement of accounts, which really was an accounting practice designed to aid cash flow. However, even discounting policies are a form of sales promotion, still widely used today to gain a competitive edge.

These were the "golden days" of mass markets, and any concept of an organized and planned promotional strategy was as yet unheard of. Now, mass markets have largely disappeared, to be replaced by more narrowly segmented product categories. This has meant that producers face consumers, once happy with general purpose products, who now want specialized items, bringing a huge increase in the competition for consumers' disposable income. A good example of this can be seen in the US, where the SAMI market research company reported that the number of cereal brands with sales of more than $1bn grew from 84 in the late 1970s to 150 just ten years later. Equally, the number of toothpaste brands sold in food stores rose during the same period from 10 to 31.[1]

Brands that once were dominant in their field have been forced to add new variants and versions of themselves to defend their market leadership against new competitors able to cater for those who demand ever-tighter specifications. A good illustration of this proliferation is the detergent brand Persil. In the 1960s, this brand dominated the market in the UK with a share of around 33%. It had one single-pack design, the only variation being in the size of the packs, catering for different-sized families and purses. Today, most supermarkets will have Persil in any number of versions (along with other brands) to cater for a bewildering number of demands. This makes for many difficulties when it comes to promoting Persil and a version of it – so that users and prospects are left in no doubt as to what is being promoted and for what purpose – as well as deciding any promotional inducements that may accompany them.

Service providers are subject to this segmentation just as much as companies with physical products. Good examples of this are financial service companies, especially the high-street banks. Not too many years ago, opening a bank account was a relatively simple affair and the banks went out of their way to present themselves as being friendly and unstuffy. (The fact that they are still trying to make us see this indicates the size of the task they have.) Customers were given check facilities, details on interest-carrying deposits, and that was about it. Now, banks have become money marketers, and new customers opening an account are faced with a tariff of charges requiring the calculations of a computer, and an enormous variety of services ranging from mortgages to insurance to credit/debit card offerings.

It is not just functional differences that can influence the process of market segmentation. Psychological and emotional needs act as strongly as any other when it comes to choice. Think for a moment of all those motorists who drive vast off-road vehicles; the nearest these vehicles ever get to being off-road is when they are standing on the owners' driveways. What counts here is the aspiration that many people have for a lifestyle forever beyond their personal limitations. Nevertheless, we have yet another segment of a large market, catering for those who perhaps wish to be perceived as coming from a landed estate.

Such market segmentation is ongoing. One only has to look at the market for electronic "toys" and gadgets to realize how far and how fast this growing market has come within a mere handful of years. Just a decade ago the sale of mobile telephones was minimal, due in large part to the extraordinary weight of the power packs that had to be carried to allow them to function. Now the market is probably nearing saturation point and manufacturers are desperately promoting new variants, extra features, and tariffs that confuse buyers more than they clarify. The same can be said of the market for computers, where makers are only too anxious to promote an exciting new product or program to give them an important edge in this valuable industry. Such is the rush to innovate that the product you buy today is probably already out of date in technical terms. But this, of course, is part of the psychology of promoting to people the idea that they should constantly be updating their hardware if they are to be at the leading edge in their own business sector.

The market, which started out being "mass," is now breaking down, almost to individual level, whereby requirements are virtually tailored to suit needs and wants. This is seen clearly when one looks at the groups who can be promoted to, for example housewives who also do paid work, teenage girls, pensioners, ethnic minorities, homosexual men, or food faddists. Add to this phenomenon the fact that people are far more mobile in their lifestyles than was ever the case, and also in their use of disposable income, and it will be appreciated that marketing has undergone a seismic shift in the 60 or 70 years since it was first really thought about, as has the role that sales promotion has had to perform during the same period.

When there was a mass market (e.g. in the days when Persil came in just one design pack) it was relatively easy to promote or sell to that sector. A number of important changes, as we have noted, have altered the way manufacturers and suppliers of services are able to communicate to market segments. Once it was feasible to run a television campaign across the country, as in the 1950s when there was just one terrestrial channel taking advertisements in the UK; now there are three, since Channel 5 came on air. With the advent of cable and satellite channels there are more opportunities to advertise than ever before, and with more and more homes around the world equipped to take any number of channels, plus an increase in the number of hours of broadcasting open to viewers, there has been a change in the advertising budget allocated to this medium. Also, the cost of television airtime has risen more quickly than that of other advertising media.

It is not just the electronic media which have seen huge increases in advertising rates, or have proliferated, as can be witnessed by the increase in printed titles over the past few years, dealing with a rising tide of consumer specialist interests. Add in the "free sheets" that plop (uninvited) through our mailboxes and the commercial radio stations, again appealing very carefully to their target audiences, and it does not take long to realize that there is an enormous problem for an advertiser in getting their message heard above the noise and clutter of what is going on.

The advertising media today have to create themes to appeal to the segmented audiences discussed above, many of them highly specialized. Now that modern technology can arm viewers with advertisement cut-out facilities (or that people just don't watch commercials as they zap between channels) and that the expense of mounting anything like a truly national campaign is exceptionally great, the cost-efficiency of media advertising, especially television, has declined sharply over the last five to six years. This is true of almost every country where there is freedom to advertise on commercial channels.

THE "NEW" MARKETING PHILOSOPHY

Many marketing executives were brought up on the idea that a company needed to win a market share in a clearly defined market and had to do this in the face of others who had exactly the same notion. This meant, in essence, a marketing war with each side bringing ever more resources to bear. Indeed, the whole language of marketing is littered with references to military activity. It was, in the early days of marketing and sales promotion, a war of attrition as each side sought to win a market share of a point or two. But, as will be discussed later, not all marketing or sales promotion wars are fought merely to retain or gain a market share. Simply throwing ever increasing funds at the situation is not the only workable or best solution available to right-thinking businesses who are experiencing any one of a number of trading problems.

It was the Japanese who showed the world that market penetration and, in some cases, dominance could be achieved by looking at things through a different lens. Considering that Japan started from scratch at the end of World War II, how did they come so far and so fast in the areas in which they excel? Japanese companies did not have the vast funds to throw about that American and European companies had available and by rights they should never have survived, let alone become dominant, in the war for market share. Given that they were also operating in countries with different languages, cultures, and trading methods, their success in the car, electronics, and computer markets is even more astounding.

Their secret weapon was nothing really terribly exciting, apart from the fact that in the days when the Japanese were invading foreign markets, the word "quality" had not been overemployed in Western manufacturing concerns. The Japanese realized that they could not, nor would they want to, compete financially, but would offer a quality product at a fair price, backed with an excellent aftersales service. The secret, if there was one, was to spend what you had wisely, creating values which were not just perceived, but which were very real. Promoting quality, price, and delivery on time is of course the cornerstone of all good businesses – the Japanese traded on them and dragged the rest of the world up to their high standards. Some cynics would say that there is still a gap.

THE POWER OF RETAILERS

It is undeniably the case that many retailers today are much larger in size, and have more financial clout, than their suppliers. Not surprisingly, suppliers have complained that they have had their margins pared to the bone and that the big retailers are abusing their strength and power. The argument goes that it is the manufacturers who need the margins to allow them to develop new products that the retailers want to sell. Also there is little margin left for manufacturers to promote and advertise, whether independently or in conjunction with the retailer. The problem for suppliers is that, whereas a retailer may purchase, say, 20% of their output, this could represent a tiny fraction of the retailer's overall sales, further diminishing the influence of manufacturers.

The more enlightened marketing and sales promotion executives of the current generation realize that the days of manufacturers' dominance are long gone and that retailers are just as good, if not better, at sales promotion and overall marketing than those who seek to cling to the old ways of doing things. This has reached the stage where many leading retailers have become, in the minds of their regular shoppers, the natural home of trust and confidence in what is being promoted and sold – "trust" and "confidence" being the two words of course that every supplier sought to convey in their brand.

While stores are concerned with convenience, distribution, and choice, they are increasingly becoming aware of the vital need to present their wares in the best possible light – this now applies to clothes stores, white and brown goods stores, and even DIY stores – where once it was considered enough just to pile the goods high with some "exciting" come-on banner showing an equally exciting "low" price. Presentation is the name of the game and this can be seen in many of the leading multiple stores around the world where speciality sections have been created to capture the interest of both regular buyers and prospects. The use of scanning devices gives even more power to the retailers, as they soon know which items are moving well and should be further supported with promotional activity, and which should be dropped or, at least, left to be milked without being given any promotional boost. Now, in many cases, it is the retailer rather than the manufacturer who spends more heavily on advertising and engages in dialogue with their market, especially in the fast-moving consumer goods sector.

THE MANUFACTURER AND SALES PROMOTION TODAY

Although it may seem that the manufacturer has lost out in the war with the retail sector, all is not quite as straightforward as that, for while retailers have been spending conspicuously more on advertising, manufacturers have spent more on sales promotion. Why should this be so? There are a number of very important reasons and explanations.

Advertising is still regarded as the best way for promoting "the brand," whereas sales promotion is seen as the most useful way to hustle a product into a crowded marketplace. Not only that but quite a few products have been banned from some media (e.g. cigarettes and hard liquor in the UK) or restrictions have been imposed by national or international bodies as to what can be advertised, to whom, and when, making the impact almost worthless (e.g. toy advertising in Sweden, allowed only during certain hours on evening television). Moreover, the sheer cost of television or printed advertising has, for smaller companies, become prohibitive and the squeeze by retailers has left little funding anyway for them to mount any form of useful advertising campaign, at least in the fast-moving consumer goods markets.

On the positive side, promotional support to retailers can more readily be tailored and budgeted for, and the results more accurately calculated. As the available outlets for products also become more fragmented, there cannot usually be one all-embracing approach to marketing a firm's output and it is therefore sensible to have a more flexible promotional system which can take advantage of situations quickly and profitably for both parties. Many techniques which are available to promoters are discussed in Chapter 6.

Now it can be seen why there has been such a remarkable shift away from advertising to sales promotion over the last 10 years and why sales promotion now accounts for more expenditure than television and other media combined. This trend is set to continue as markets break down even further, with the knowledge gained by refined market research techniques making it easier and less wasteful to target customers and prospects far more accurately than ever. Retailers have assumed the role, therefore, that manufacturers once thought would be their own for all time. They now speak to their buyers and have, as a result, established a more cozy and influential relationship with them than the manufacturers ever achieved.

Although many people regard sales promotion activity as taking place only in the retail sector, especially in the food sector, they would be quite surprised to learn that there is virtually no business, industry, or organization which does not use some type of promotion to try to capture interest and make people do something positive as a result. This includes capital equipment, not-for-profit organizations such as charities and churches, and consumer durables (furniture, white and brown goods, cars, etc.). Even local government uses quite sophisticated promotion techniques to get across some aspects of policy that may otherwise go unnoticed or unimplemented. Some local authorities in the UK offer special discount incentives to residents to pay their community charges by direct debit or more quickly, while others organize competitions with prizes to encourage speedy or prompt payment.

SALES PROMOTION: TACTICS AND STRATEGY

At this point, while discussing the evolution of sales promotion, it is perhaps important to see how the activity has been developed with regard to tactics and strategy. Sales promotion is seen as one of the short-term, tactical "weapons" available to businesses. Certainly, it can achieve immediate effects, as campaigns can be swiftly mounted and results be counted in a few weeks. This requires that companies have a number of schemes ready to implement, but it also demands that these organizations have the ability, speed, and resources to react fast to competition and seize the short-term market opportunities that they will help to create.

No one could argue that everything in business benefits from being planned strategically. However, there are several reasons for adopting a strategic stance to the planning of sales promotions, one of which is that the next promotion can be built on the hoped-for success of the last one. Moreover, this approach helps communicate long-term brand values to the target market, in terms of making promotion work harder and be more efficient and effective. Additionally, there should be visible benefits manifested in time and money saved, not forgetting a greater speed achieved in response times, which could have a profound effect on the way promotions are designed and operated. Here are some of the more important strategic elements that should be considered.

» Understand the overall strategic framework in terms of competitive advantage and positioning – these should be the foundation of every promotion.
» Ensure that each product/brand/service has the right style of promotion, i.e. the most appropriate for it. You would seldom see a premium-priced product promoted with a "Now only £..." style of price tag or ticket, as this would destroy the brand's image.
» Get senior people to oversee every promotion to ensure that a high degree of professionalism is incorporated in the whole structure of it.
» Make sure each promotion is thoroughly researched and evaluated to discover whether it was the best way to spend precious funds. What could have been the alternatives?
» Make sure that by planning and setting budgets for promotions for at least the year ahead, they become an integral part of the overall marketing effort and not some bolted-on activity or an afterthought. Try to have two or three promotions in the pipeline for rapid development, should there be a sudden need to run one.

The following timeline highlights the innovative tactics and strategies of various entrepreneurs in the more recent history of sales promotion, as well as the inevitable legal restraints and bodies that have come in their wake.

» 1862 – The Johnson brothers, grocers of Islington in London, gave away a free journal, *The Family Grocer*.

» 1869 – Henry John Heinz, an American gardener, founded a company devoted to the manufacture and sale of horseradish. By the end of the nineteenth century, he had built this into a major food-processing company. Heinz was a great promoter, giving away samples for free home trial.

» 1879 – Frank Woolworth opened 2 five-and-ten stores in the US. In the decade that followed, he opened a further 21 stores, so becoming the first mass retailer.
  – In the same year, the first recorded cigarette card was used in Canada.

» 1880s – Jesse Boot, founder of the British chemist chain Boots, experimented with novel sales promotion ideas. These included price deals and staff opening tin cans for customers, many of whom did not possess can openers.

» 1884 – Michael Marks opened his first Penny Bazaar in Leeds in the north of England. This later expanded to become the retail chain Marks & Spencer.

» 1933 – The Sales Promotion Executives Association was formed in the UK, becoming the Institute of Sales Promotion in 1979.

» 1947 – The Co-op opened the first supermarket in the UK. This heralded a new era of self-service and sales promotion. Plastic flowers at the cash till formed a new concept in promotional terms.

» 1960s – The Esso Tiger in your Tank and Shell Make Money, two of the most successful promotions ever, were launched.

» 1962 – The Advertising Standards Authority was formed in the UK.
  – In the same year, the first edition of the British Codes of Advertising and Sales Promotion Practice was issued.

» 1968 – The Gaming Act 1968, which seeks to regulate games of chance, was passed in the UK.

» 1976 – The Lotteries and Amusements Act 1976, which seeks to regulate prize promotions, was passed in the UK.

» 1992 – The Hoover promotion began, which has become a cause célèbre in the history of sales promotion for the repercussions it created for many years and which are still being felt now.

» 1996 – Coca-Cola ran a promotion in the Philippines with a $1mn prize to be claimed via a single can holding the winning details. However, by mistake, two cans held the winning details and two people were shot dead in the ensuing riots that took place in Manila.

NOTES

1 Petersen, C. and Toop, A. (1994) *Sales Promotion in Postmodern Marketing*. Gower, Aldershot.

The E-Dimension of Sales Promotion

» The growth and use of e-business.
» The take-up and use of e-business in sales promotion.
» Changes in purchasing habits – intangible/physical products.
» Examples of e-promotions, including best practice.
» Is e-promotion right for your product/service? – the medium is the message.

There is no doubt that e-business and everything that stems from it has caused organizations to take a fresh look at the ways in which they communicate with their markets over the past three or four years. The British monthly *E-Business Review* has some interesting statistics on the use of e-business in its February, 2001 issue.[1] Of those responding to a questionnaire, 80% said that it would help simplify buying and selling, 75% said that it would help establish new partnerships, and 22% said that it would improve inventory management. That was on the positive side.

The negative side revealed that 42% thought there would be loss of personal contact, 33% believed there would be more complicated transactions, 10% reckoned there would be loss of brand differentiation, and 71% assumed there would be loss of competitive advantage. However, over 80% of manufacturers said they would be using e-business in the marketplace by the year 2002, as did 45% of retailers, especially when it came to promoting niche products.

So now there is a "new" form of marketing and sales promotion available – e-marketing. As with many innovations that create huge interest when they first appear, people believe that they will radically alter the way our lives and businesses are conducted. What they do in reality is to make life perhaps a little easier or allow organizations to gather and process data more quickly and efficiently. The telephone, electrical appliances, the fax, the photocopier, and the computer have not done away with the things that were once done by hand or by personal visits, as the fax still only sends copies of documents and computers are merely able to perform more quickly functions once laboriously undertaken by squads of staff.

The Internet is, in effect, an alternative method of communication, albeit one that is near instant and still relatively novel. How then is the Internet influencing sales promotion and e-marketing, since it is still regarded as somewhat untried, compared to the more familiar systems? As has been mentioned, manufacturers and retailers are rapidly taking up e-business and one of the main uses will be for customer acquisition and retention, for one-to-one marketing, just like a direct mail letter, only sent electronically. Consumers are encouraged to ask for information on products they would like to hear about. For example, a music store gets people to check boxes that describe the music they like. They are then asked whether they would like to receive information on a need-to-know basis. So a "new" promotional/marketing tool has been developed.

The idea can be extended quite easily for "retention e-mail," which exploits the data already held by a company. Then there is "sponsorship e-mail," which is an alternative to buying online advertising, a sort of successor to banner advertising as it begins an e-mail-based relationship with the prospect. The downside is that, while the surfer has opted in to receiving the e-mail, there is no previous relationship to build on, and relationship marketing is vital for businesses where customer loyalty is paramount.

According to the US research company Forrester, the e-mail marketing industry will be worth around $5bn worldwide by 2004 and each online household will receive on average nine marketing e-mails a day. How many times will the delete key be hit, though? Users click on advertisements as many as 10 times more than they do on banners. How will promoters view this in their overall thinking? (Note: The EU wants to update data protection laws to to outlaw unsolicited e-mails and, as a result, there could be a major clash with the commercial sector.)

What of the other "new" technologies and shopping habits? And how will all this impact on sales promotion? Interactive TV is of little interest currently as it is seen to be too dear and too technically limited, while mobile phones, WAPs phones and other systems have yet to prove they have anything real to offer promoters, who are looking for the right media on which to spend their strictly limited budgets. It is reckoned that few shoppers will shift their entire traditional purchasing methods to the Internet for any group of physical products. What will increase is the amount of gambling (because of legislation) and share dealing (because of costs). No doubt promoters and companies in these two sectors have already taken steps to capitalize on this promotional opportunity.

Of the people who do shop/buy online, 50% are men and 50% are women. They tend to be upmarket folk, free-spending and with credit cards. The problem that retailers have is that they have not yet cracked the relationship management problem and they are having to learn that it is not solved by throwing huge amounts of money at it. Additionally, the question of security – of data and payment – has yet to be satisfactorily solved to create the sense of trust and confidence so important in business. This has been a seriously limiting factor in the growth of the medium, in spite of the fact that there are excellent measures in place which should have reduced the risks to virtually nil by now. As with all forms of advertising, it is important to be seen to be promoting/advertising in the medium which best reflects your company, its products, and its brand image. Not only that but it must also carry the most appropriate message for your company in that medium, so that it will not harm what has probably taken years to build in the minds of your public.

In the UK, stores that have succeeded with their shopping online are Tesco, Sainsbury, Asda/Wal-Mart, Iceland, and Waitrose. Tesco e-mails customers with information and provides e-coupons to be spent in-store or online! Those stores that could not cut the mustard include Somerfield and Budgens, as they found that it was too costly to promote online and the returns were insufficient.

In the US, Internet users are exceptionally keen on contests, as they are easy to enter online. Treasure hunts, trivia tests, quizzes, and surveys are also popular, as are hyperlinks that send users to a different random Website every time they are clicked on. An example of a successful online contest is that organized by DealerNet – a virtual showroom selling new and used cars across the US. They gave away a car to the winner, but the effect was incredible as the Usenet newsgroups hummed with people swapping the URL (Uniform Resource Locator) for the online entry form. The promotion hit the media headlines, which further added to its success.

Also successful was the online book competition run by Random House Juvenile Publishing, in which $5000 was offered to the person writing the best final chapter. Strangely, the competition did less well the second time around – even though the prize money was doubled to $10,000. There is a simple lesson to be learned here: sales promotions have to be seen to be fresh and novel. Rehashing a once successful idea is no guarantee of further successes.

One of the most popular contest sites is Riddler (www.riddler.com) where browsers can participate in several advertiser-supported trivia games and treasure hunts. Some Webmasters have included treasure hunts in their own sites. To get more people to explore more of your Website, consider hiding something and giving a prize to those who find it or entering them in a monthly draw. Prompting people to fill out a survey by offering to enter them in a contest should encourage an even higher level of participation.

Here are 10 tips for running your own e-promotions.

1 Design your promotion so that you don't exclude AOL or Macintosh, or out-of-date Web browsers.
2 Design your promotion for utility rather than for entertainment.
3 Consider whether your target audience is online. People need two things to participate in an e-promotion – a computer and (usually) an account with an online service, which could exclude a huge number, leaving you with those who are unlikely to join in.
4 Decide what you are going to measure. Site traffic? Sales? Enquiries? Then calculate what percentage conversion rate you need to make it worthwhile. Remember the importance of brand recognition, goodwill, and cachet or image. Should your product or company even be seen being involved in a promotion?
5 A good e-promotion is called "content" online and there are many Websites starved of good content. So go where the traffic is with the big sites that always need good content and leave the technical details to them.
6 The top Internet sites are dominated by Internet directories (and adult boards), so use sense before you decide to partner with anyone. Co-branding with a directory service is a good idea but remember they are not destination sites. So consider Hot Wired, Playboy, ESPNet, Family Planet, etc. These include directories, chat rooms, news, features, and stores, drawing large numbers daily. However, it is vital to distinguish "views," "visitors," and "clicks!"
7 Check whether the site is workable and has good content. Does it have quality illustrations, talented writers, and name recognition? Does it inspire trust, have good communication, handle problems well and, if children are your target market, does it market to children? Is it easy to understand or is it so complex that it turns people away?
8 Franchise your traffic builder to other sites or ask for a graphical hotlink to your site directly from the gimmick. That way you get brand recognition, but only from visitors who are interested in your product and not just the gimmick.

9 Look for ad banners that appear only when someone does a search containing certain words, say *travel*, *holiday*, *tickets*, etc.
10 Look to see whether you can go online with a promotion linked to a special event, e.g. an exhibition, trade show, sports event, etc. (This will be covered in Chapter 7.)

BEST PRACTICE: RANDOM HOUSE

Here is an example of a good e-promotion. Random House Juvenile Publishing launched an interactive promotion titled "The Lurker Files." This was a fictional online college with a chat room called the Rats Keller where the Lurker lay in wait. Behind it all was a professional story-writer who spun out stories about fictional characters and invited comments from Website visitors. It was co-branded (jointly promoted) with Yahoo, one of the biggest Internet companies. They created Yahooligans, a catalog for children, and there was a premium spot on the Yahoo entertainment page.

Random House included a contest whereby children were invited to write a fictional account of living online. In this instance the prize was not money, as in the book promotion mentioned earlier, but *fame*. The effects of this promotion were far-reaching – teachers used it to encourage essay-writing and the use of good English – beyond all the merchandise that was marketed in connection with the promotion (i.e. more books, clothing, and related children's items). The promotion was able to run for many months as interest built up and more people participated. This is one of the few times that any form of sales promotion can afford to allow people more than a month in which to take part, as usually the fatigue factor negates the excitement initially generated. Of course the skill of the professional writer who was able to maintain a high level of interest played an enormously important part.

Key words and ideas which emerge from this promotion:

» *integrity* – all parties have it;
» *appeal* – excellent for children;
» *scope* – covers the target market well;

» *timing* – when to run it and for how long has to be finely calculated;
» *novelty* – certainly different; and
» *preparation* – always spend more time on preparation than any other part of a promotion; it pays to get it right at the very beginning.

TOP TIPS FOR RUNNING E-PROMOTIONS

» Look for that flash of inspiration.
» Get the right partner if working with another party.
» Creativity is so important – remember Marshall McLuhan's dictum "the medium is the message," i.e. consider whether you should you be online at all with a promotion.
» Make sure you define your target audience as accurately as possible.
» Allow at least twice the amount of time you had originally budgeted for preparation – to get it right!
» Decide the criteria for measuring success.

Useful link

» Top 100 Websites: www.pcmag.com/special/web100/topt.htm

NOTES

1 *E-Business Review*, February, 2001.

The Global Dimension of Sales Promotion

» Factors influencing international promotions.
» Promoting in a single country abroad.
» Multiple-country promotions.
» Sales promotion without borders.
» Best practice.

By clicking on to various Websites, it is possible to believe that sales promotions can quite easily cross the world. And when we speak about international promotions, we perhaps think of major worldwide activity with a branded product being promoted in any number of individual countries at the same time and using an agreed theme that can easily translate. A truly international promotion should be able to appear in many countries and not have to run at precisely the same time or carry exactly the same format.

Usually an international promotion starts off with a successful promotion run in one country. The sales promotion world, just like many industries, is a relatively small village and talk of a successful scheme soon gets picked up by sales promotion agencies, with the result that it is run – with few changes – by the same company overseas or by a competitor. Obviously the originating company wants to maximize the effectiveness and reduce the cost basis of its international promotional operations, and therefore the overriding consideration is money. Apart from keeping origination charges down, there are several other factors that can be influenced if a promotion can be made "global," all in the end having a financial as well as a promotional benefit.

» If a promotion offers a special premium item in return for cash, coupons, or whatever, then a better deal could be struck with the supplier, handler, and distributor.
» If internationally known characters from television, books, etc. are to be used, then it makes sense to negotiate globally for their use.
» Likewise, if real celebrities are being featured, then arranging international rights makes financial sense. (Note: Take care when using any sporting, TV, film, or other celebrity, as they can bring disaster if they become involved with activities which don't square with your company's image, or fail to perform to their usual high standards.)

Apart from these considerations, pressure from a corporate point of view may suggest that it is best for international promotional schemes to be handled where there is the most expertise, rather than allow regional offices to implement something that may be out of their "local" league. The big worry that stalks these corporates is that their precious international brand identity and image may, in some way, be blighted by a lack of professional capabilities. As has been seen, the increasing importance of sales promotion in the marketing mix, and the ever rising number of media for carrying it, has led many companies to the conclusion that sales promotion can no longer be regarded as a local activity supported by a limited amount of cross-border information-swapping.

What emerged during the late 1990s were two distinct forms for international promotion design and development, as it was not every product or brand that could be promoted universally with the same idea. The first form does hold to the view that for them one promotion worldwide does the job, e.g. Coca-Cola and Pepsi. The second form recognizes that this approach cannot work because of local customs, taboos, laws, etc. and so creates promotional solutions which will suit a number of countries. As long as a company sticks as closely as possible to the global theme, then it can allow the local details to be accommodated to incorporate the company culture. The difference between the two forms is best summed up by two words – *control* and *delegation*. What cannot be denied is the benefit derived from the economy of scale.

PROMOTING IN A SINGLE COUNTRY ABROAD

Basically, promoting in a country overseas is little different from promoting in the UK or your home territory. You must still know about the people there, how they do business, what their lifestyle is like, what their aspirations are, and just what the law there allows with regard to sales promotion. Think about the timing, religion (especially religious breaks), the climate, distribution, local media to support the promotion, and how you will actually implement and control the scheme away from base. Also consider whether there is sufficient professionalism in the country to cope with the scheme, a point illustrated by one Central European country that ran a promotion for a brand of tea, resulting in the nation's post office being so overwhelmed with applications that it had to close down to clear the backlog of mail.

MULTIPLE-COUNTRY PROMOTIONS

It is a truism to say "keep it simple." If you are planning to run a promotion across a number of countries, then you would be wise to keep it as simple as possible. One of the world's largest oil companies went global with a promotion that was designed to reinforce the company's sponsorship of a Formula One motor-racing team. The idea was to allow the petrol stations to give out model racing cars in the most appropriate way, either by redeeming them against oil or petrol sales, or by discounting them for cash against smaller purchases. The promotion gave the participants freedom to use the main theme while enjoying local license.

There are other schemes that have a pan-European or even global appeal, such as major sporting events (e.g. soccer or the Olympic Games) and major charity operations (e.g. The Red Cross). However, these types of schemes need to be very carefully planned and cleared locally before they are allowed to be run, as unintentional embarrassment could be caused should local involvement not be taken into consideration. But never let a really good, internationally sound promotion idea be spoiled by local management, who want to run something inferior because of the "not-invented-here" syndrome!

Now that the world is becoming more regionalized into trading blocks, with laws and business practices becoming increasingly harmonized, it is quite likely that sales promotions will operate on a more "multi-country" basis rather than go global or remain purely national.

SALES PROMOTION WITHOUT BORDERS

The Internet has shown how rapidly the world has shrunk, metaphorically speaking, bringing in its wake all manner of new approaches to the old problem of trying to find something different to attract the attention of the selected marketplace. The vast army of business travellers touring the world for any one of a dozen reasons tend to stay at similar hotels, fly on similar airlines, use similar photographic film and equipment, drink similar drinks, and so on. The suppliers of these products and services are obviously keen to capture new clients and then keep them loyal. As many hotel groups are now global operators, they will design sales promotions geared to their needs and tailored to their corporate lifestyle. Maybe the only thing that needs to be changed is the language but, as English seems to be the international language, maybe even that is not necessary. Indeed, in some cases, it is seen as a most distinctive approach, according a special cachet to both promoter and customer.

Other borderless activities can be mounted by such well-known organizations as McDonald's (who have over 22,000 outlets globally), Benetton, Kodak, and Nestlé, with maybe a touch of the local flavour to make the activities work and with regard to national laws and culture. Never forget that the local distributors and retail outlets will respond in different ways in different countries and may require various levels of support to help maximize the effectiveness of the sales promotion.

Pareto's Theory states that 80% of business is produced by 20% of customers. By the same token, only 20% of promotions succeed, leaving 80% to fail. Many of the failures were perhaps not poor promotions in themselves but failed, nevertheless, because of a failure to plan adequately. The fact that a promotion is about to be launched in another country, in another region, or globally should alert planners to the increased chances of failure or at least the hazards that lie ahead.

The first step for an international promoter is to check carefully that what you are about to execute is legal in that territory. For example, in Germany you cannot offer anything that is not product-related and not worth more than a small percentage of the original article. You can run a competition or a sweepstake, but not a free draw. In a competition, the answers must be easy to find on the competition form and you may then award the prize to the first correct entry received – a free draw in all but name. But don't have the entry form too near the product to which it is related.

If you are promoting in the Middle East, have a care for the differences in attitudes to women, money, prizes, and alcohol. Again, make sure that any representation of people (i.e. the portrayal of color, sex, attitudes, and lifestyle in print or the media) does nothing to upset local cultures, and ensure that no colors are employed which could give rise to offence. For example, in the Far East white signifies death, while in parts of Africa gold is a symbol of wealth and green a symbol of fertility.

Having prepared the ground for the right style of promotion, colors, and support materials, it is essential to know that there are really good, not just adequate, back-up services. This means that participating dealers, distributors, retailers, and other parties involved are fully briefed and that handling houses checking coupons or redemptions are up to the task. While we may complain about some of the problems experienced with the Royal Mail in the UK, these are as nothing compared to the postal services of some other countries, as mentioned earlier. It is worth knowing what might go wrong in this area, so as to avoid problems with your company's image should anything go adrift. If the promotion involves a special give-away or premium item, it is worth checking to see whether the local customs have a say in it and what duties could be levied. Get a local agent to help smooth the way.

Finally, when deciding on an award to participants, it is always advisable to find out if the local culture is supportive of an instant reward – might the people be happier to join in a collector-type scheme? In developing countries the usual requirement is for instant gratification, as the people live for the "now." Find those who know the answers to the questions you have to ask before you make any moves, and design your sales promotion with this information in mind. International or global sales promoters will soon build up a "book of experience" and a data bank of those who have the right international expertise to tap into. It is better to spend money on getting it right before the promotion begins than to have to spend a great deal more in trying to sort it out if things start to go wrong.

Although many economies, especially Western ones, do not now rely so much on individual counter service, there are plenty of countries where this style of service is still normal. This means that a promotion that was once popular or successful some years ago in the age of personal service could still be used in other countries, but check out the pitfalls before launching it abroad.

BEST PRACTICE: READER'S DIGEST

Sales promotion offers can be based on motivation, and can happily exploit situations and subjects that are just as internationally appealing as those used in above-the-line advertising. Just as advertising can have an international theme, so too can sales promotion as already described.

Reader's Digest is a publication that is known in many parts of the world, printed in several languages, and that relies heavily on a number of sales promotion techniques, not only to retain the continuing loyalty of subscribers but also to attract new ones to the wider range of publications. Many of its publisher's more expensive books are genuinely excellent, both in content and in value. To promote them to its market, Reader's Digest uses a series of heavy-hitting direct mailings to its own membership list and to specially bought-in ones giving the right kind of readership profile.

It is not just the sheer weight of mailings that the company is so well known for; the variations on the "winning" theme set this organization apart from any other that has a relatively high-ticket item to promote and sell. The contents of each envelope are designed to lead prospects through a fairly complex routine, aided by a huge amount of personalization in the text of the copy. The envelope itself is almost a marketing work of art as it too has been carefully worded to capture instant attention, with promises that the receiver is already guaranteed a place in the third round of a draw to win X amount of money, a home, or some other major award, which can be had merely by completing the right paperwork contained in the envelope.

Each document has a degree of authority invested in it, with high-sounding titles for the executives in charge, special colors, and certificates with your name emblazoned in high-profile places. There is enough important-looking and impressive-sounding paperwork that, on reading it through, together with the special sample sheet, you are inclined to overlook the price or how to pay for the goods, so that your name is entered in the next section of the prize draw. The various techniques that have been used include rub-off gold foil to see if your reference matches the printed one, keys to match locks, and many other similar small "tests." The main thing to remember about Reader's Digest draws is that everyone can enter, whether you are a buyer or not, but non-purchaser entries go into a separate pile! Early responders are also deemed to be priority, able to take advantage of an even bigger prize than those who dawdled before submitting their paperwork. The success of this approach would appear to fly in the face of anecdotal evidence, which suggests that few people bother to take up the offers and respond to the allure of the massive winnings on offer. However, with such a large mailing, backed with exciting offers and prizes, even a 2% or 3% response will probably bring the commercial reward looked for.

One of the most remembered of all Reader's Digest promotions was based on sending two cents to a specially selected audience, representing the change from say $2 (for a $1.98 deal). The concept was used for a number of promotions with a few variations for many years until, in the end, it became too difficult to deal with the mailings returning the coins and the US Post Office refused to destroy them. So the company contacted a boys' club which wanted to build a new clubhouse and asked them to help. The boys opened up the returned mail and put the coins into two piles, one of which they kept for their new building. The other pile was for reuse! History records that something like 50 million coins were involved and the publication became the very first private customer of the US Mint.

The secret of such good schemes is to make them simple, fun, and rewarding, no matter where in the world they are operated. The major premise with Reader's Digest is that for a modest outlay on one of their publications you could be a winner on a grand scale, and that even the lower-ranked prizes are still handsome. And look, we've even got you through the first three rounds so there is every incentive to go the whole way! Good psychology. Plus the fact that your promotional campaign should have brought in a whole new generation of readers, which was one of the aims in the first place.

The State of The Art in Sales Promotion

- » The need for quality control.
- » Promotional partnerships.
- » Why do promoters promote?
- » The mnemonic *SMART*.
- » Promotional needs.
- » The 10 objectives that sales promotion can meet.
- » Strategic hierarchies.
- » Types of sales promotions – value/price and instant/delayed.
- » The Hoover saga.
- » Budget, timing, and communication.
- » Legal matters.
- » Using outside suppliers – the need to use them.
- » The future.

It has been said that sales promotion is merely bribery. This is admittedly a rather biased and jaundiced opinion, but it will no doubt have support in some quarters where the proper understanding of free enterprise and commercial instincts is not terribly well developed or is totally lacking. It is true that both marketing and promotions have been subjected to criticism from time to time, as there has been a great deal of waste and silly or even trivial activity characterizing the whole discipline. A highly responsible attitude is vital and will become increasingly more so if the knockers are to be silenced or or at least kept quieter. This requires that, for the first time, many promoters will be forced to look at "quality control" and "total quality control" if they are to remain players in the fast-growing use of the activity which, sadly, still has some misusers and abusers. So what are the benefits to companies which practice total quality in sales promotion?

» The "get it right first time" idea will help reduce errors and costs.
» The timescale required for planning can be reduced.
» Commitment will be improved.
» Customer/supplier partnerships will improve.
» Promotions will be designed to be more in keeping with customer needs.

If these few pointers are applied solely to the sales promotion world, then there are even more benefits for companies to consider:

» promotions will come in on budget;
» no more illegal promotion schemes;
» no rush jobs involving premium rate payments;
» clearer instructions to all participants;
» few or no complaints;
» prizes/rewards delivered on time;
» proper evaluation systems, so that errors can be avoided in future;
» more successful promotions; and (last but most important)
» more satisfied customers.

Over the past few years many companies have found that it pays to have the accreditation of the British Standards Institution (in particular BS 5750) and the International Standards Organization (especially ISO

9000). Manufacturers have found that, in order even to be invited to tender for jobs, they have to be certified by one of these bodies, as this bestows on them the level of quality that is deemed necessary in today's business climate. More and more service companies, including sales promotion agencies, are applying for this accreditation.

Partnerships are also being formed as never before in many areas, not least in sales promotion. The benefits can be summed up as:

» shared values – there are no illusions as to the targets for the promotion;
» closer understanding of each other's working practices;
» no hidden or personal agendas;
» good, long-term relationships can be established; and
» results will be more easily and widely accepted by all parties, and improvements put in hand more readily if needed.

If total quality and all that it stands for is instituted, then a way of working that delivers the best results can be built upon. But the one thing that has to be remembered is that any promotion should begin with a clear brief for a well-defined promotional need. First a question needs to be posed, then answered, namely: "Why do promoters promote?" Naturally there is more than one answer, and here are just four of the most common (and true) ones.

1 The account executive wants to make a splash and raise their profile before moving on to another job.
2 There is quite a lot of budget still to be spent this year.
3 The sales people desperately need something bright and fresh to talk to their customers about.
4 A specific marketing need has been noted that can best be addressed by a sales promotion or be included in a suitable strategy.

The latter is of course the real reason for implementing any promotion. Chris Brown, in his book on sales promotion, claims that the objective of any promotion should use the mnemonic *SMART*: *S* for *specific*, *M* for *measurable*, *A* for *achievable*, *R* for *relevant*, *T* for *timed* or *timing*.[1] Taking a closer look at these five words:

1 *Specific* – focus on the real task, i.e. what the promotion is designed to do.
2 *Measurable* – you must know when and if the targets have been met, as otherwise there is no benchmark for measuring the success of the current promotion or future ones.
3 *Achievable* – while it is wise to set high targets, there is no point in setting them unrealistically high as disillusionment and apathy can set in.
4 *Relevant* – you have to ensure that the objectives set are the right ones for the brand's problems, and that the content and style of the scheme is the right one for the product or brand.
5 *Timed/timing* – it is vital that the promotion is run at the most appropriate time to coincide with a season/sales period and that it runs for a specific period over which results can be accurately determined.

Looking at the business of promotional needs in more detail, we will find that one of the most important is getting people to use a product or brand for the first time (trial), so there is also a need to make them aware of the promotion. Trial is necessary when there is a new brand or there is a major makeover or it has been repositioned in the marketplace (upgraded). Getting people to switch from their usual brand to yours will also be the task of a promotion, and it will have to be a better offer than they are currently receiving to make them desert their usual portfolio of brands. All this has to be achieved without diminishing the image of the brand or that of the company. It is quite true that it is easier for a sales promotion to have a negative rather than a positive effect on image. It is also true, on the other hand, that the best promotions deliver more than they promised and that customers recognize this. Think "quality" and it will be a great investment.

Having attracted a new customer, the objective is to keep them loyal and coming back to your brands. However, loyalty is in the customer, not the brand, and many who switch brands will seldom stay loyal for long and will be off seeking the next attractive offer. This point is hammered home in a paper by Professor Ehrenberg and two colleagues, Hammond and Goodhardt, entitled "The after-effects of consumer promotions."[2] The most important aspects of this paper were that:

» there is no before-and-after effect on sales, meaning that there is no long-lasting benefit as the result of a promotion; and
» there is hardly any discernible after-effect on customer loyalty.

Does this mean that:

» people refuse to take up the offers because they don't feel it's worth the risk?
» people don't even notice any promotion outside their normal brand purchases?

Obviously companies would never promote at the levels or frequencies that they do if there were little or no benefit to be derived from implementing them. So it is necessary to look beyond the confines of the learned gentlemen's studies to discover what motivates organizations to go to such lengths to achieve their objectives, as nobody in business is ever going to give away something for nothing.

In any debate on sales promotion there has to be a rationale stating what might, at first sight, appear to be simplistic. This rationale must cover:

» the strategic nature of the brand, that is its position in the market, its strengths and weaknesses, and any advantages over its competition;
» the real task of the promotion (see below);
» identifying the people whom you wish to influence;
» identifying what you want them to do in terms of behavior towards your brand;
» the resources that are available to achieve the targets; and
» the evaluation techniques used to measure what has happened.

There are only really 10 objectives that sales promotion can possibly and satisfactorily tackle. Any others are only extensions of the main list and these 10 will always form the key issues that surround every promotional activity in whichever industry uses it.

1 Increase volume.
2 Increase trial of the product.
3 Increase repeat purchase.

4 Increase or maintain that elusive loyalty level.
5 Widen usage of the product/service.
6 Merely create interest.
7 Generate awareness (as does advertising).
8 Deflect attention from the (real) price.
9 Gain the support of dealers, distributors, and retailers.
10 Discriminate among your users.

INCREASE VOLUME

No amount of promotion can ever hope to overcome a deficient product as its success is dependent on a number of factors, including price, quality, value and, of course, its distribution. Promotions solely geared to increasing volume (of sales), while not overcoming any of these weaknesses can, however, be of tremendous help in achieving short-term tactical needs.

With new models, preparations, and variations of existing lines, it is important to shift old stock or reduce stock levels at year ends. By the same token, it is important for consumers and stockists to increase their levels of purchasing, perhaps as a tactical ploy to spoil the launch of a competitor's new line. Price promotions are effective in the short term, as they attract the trialist as well as the regular user and can be used to break into new markets. However, a serious cut in price could send out entirely the wrong signals – that the company was desperate to shift something that was not selling. No one would ever expect to see a premium-priced car, such as a Rolls Royce, being offered at a huge discount. Additionally, price cuts can merely concertina purchases into the period of the price-cut promotion, with normal buying habits being resumed later. But at least the promoting company is "making something happen."

INCREASE TRIAL

It is a basic tenet of any business that it has to attract new prospects if it wishes to grow. Potential trialists, by definition, probably have no knowledge of you, your product, or your company. They may be happy with their current arrangements or not even be using a product in your category. To overcome their inertia, one of the following tactics could be employed.

» Give them a free sample or a coupon to try out your product.
» Let them have an extra benefit, so that trialists perceive a real difference between your product and the competition.
» Give attractive discount/credit terms to trialists.
» Run a special event or open day to bring in new prospects.

Try to be imaginative and creative so that the targeted prospects feel that their effort will be worthwhile.

INCREASE REPEAT PURCHASE

Where people chop and change the brands they buy, a promotion designed to keep them loyal will not only help stop them buying a competitor's line by bringing forward their regular purchase, but will also encourage them to buy more in bulk, which will have the added benefits of keeping out the opposition for longer, keeping customers loyal for longer, and, hopefully, turning them into long-term customers. Some simple devices to encourage this habit are:

» coupons giving money off the next purchase or off the product itself;
» the well-known BOGOF ("buy one, get one free"), or three for the price of two;
» collector schemes whereby customers collect tokens/labels off, say, ten packs/items and receive free merchandise or even a cash refund.

INCREASE LOYALTY

Many supermarkets adopted promotions that were purely designed to lock in their shoppers on a long-term basis. They have used (Green Shield) stamps, points/loyalty cards, and long-term collector schemes where a range of merchandise branded with the product can be offered without too much administration being involved.

Another good idea is to set up clubs that people join, from health and fitness clubs to those that offer special goods, e.g. wine or children's products. In the UK, the supermarket Tesco arranged a scheme that enabled schools to receive computers through the efforts over a period of its loyal customers. Everyone wins, and the good PR spin-off is an added bonus.

WIDEN USAGE

Many products are bought to fulfil a single function. But, with a clever promotion, users can be persuaded to take a fresh look at your product and use it in a novel way. The simplest example is possibly in the area of cookery where, by showing how an everyday product can be used in a new recipe, a new volume of a cookbook can be offered on the back of the basic ingredient. Drinking sherry on ice was unheard of, as was mixing it with a mixer, and it can take a lot of promotional effort, linked with good PR and advertising, to change peoples' perceptions.

CREATE INTEREST

Sales promotions should certainly create interest and try to spice up the lives of everyday shopping and buying. Manufacturers and retailers alike are constantly trying to keep their offerings fresh and interesting by changing store layouts and by offering some added benefit and fun for their customers. Jesse Boots, founder of the Boots chain, knew the value of this as he always wanted something for the shoppers to be talking about, and today we have the various activities of Richard Branson promoting the brand name Virgin. One of the most innovative was the Esso "Tiger in Your Tank" scheme, which ran for months back in the 1960s and had people driving round with a tiger's tail hanging from their filler cap. Getting a celebrity to come on board will also pay good dividends, as long as you select the correct one!

GENERATE AWARENESS

Can a sales promotion generate awareness? Yes, if you join up with another product that is already well known in its market. This is ideal for launching (or relaunching) a new product, for example coffee and a new brand of biscuit. A link with a charity or sports event could work well, e.g. a keep-fit product or shower gel and the British Olympic Association to raise funds for the athletes.

DEFLECT ATTENTION FROM PRICE

Price wars are, in the long run, the best way to play havoc with company profitability. Price is the only element in the marketing mix that actually produces revenue. All others involve costs. Usually the better approach is to offer more value, even if this means raising the price. This is less expensive to the promoting company than deep price cuts, as the product usually costs less than money-off deals. There are a number of techniques which can be employed:

» variations on the old price cut by offering so much off the next purchase, selling three for the price of two, or even doing a cash-back deal;
» offering extra in a pack, joint packs (banded packs), or some aspect of the service/product free (e.g. one hour's free consultation); and
» offering shoppers a long-term collector scheme, which is often seen as being rather more interesting than price cuts.

These schemes also have the added advantage of keeping your product users loyal, at the same time as keeping them away from your competitors.

GAIN INTERMEDIARY SUPPORT

To make a promotion work and be successful requires the wholehearted support of all the various intermediaries along the relevant distribution chain, be they retailers, agents, or distributors. Without their co-operation, the promotion would probably remain in the warehouse or store. A program geared to these important people is therefore a must. Techniques include:

» incentives aimed at store managers and sales assistants for best displays, goods shifted against target, etc.;
» price deals that generate more profit for the intermediary, higher margins on certain lines, etc.; and
» tailoring a promotion for one store group only – this is a particularly effective method as it can be tied in with some co-operative advertising with the store group to enhance the overall performance of the scheme.

There are also other ideas such as the ''member-get-member'' scheme, where customers are rewarded for bringing in new business/customers and for creating special events in which the trade can participate. These could include a golf day, or a well-organized training day together with some competitive event to spice things up.

DISCRIMINATE AMONG USERS

Many industries and service providers suffer from the fact that they are faced with a high level of fixed costs whatever the number of users. To encourage use of facilities, companies are quite happy to let certain categories of people take advantage of special rates or terms which, although they may not be as profitable, nevertheless provide what the accountants call a "contribution." Basically, this means that it is better to receive some revenue to set off against overheads than just to have those assets earning nothing. So train companies, holiday resort hotels, airlines, etc. have a wide range of tariffs which are available to customers, as long as they are prepared to tolerate certain restrictions. The skill is to ensure that those prepared to pay the full rate cannot take advantage of these deals, unless they are members of some special group that puts all its business in the hands of one organization catering for that type of activity or that operates a certain loyalty program.

THE STRATEGIC HIERARCHIES

So how does all that we have been discussing fit into the overall business program?

» First there is the *company strategy*.
» Then there is the *market strategy*.
» This is followed by the *brand strategy*.
» All this has to be condensed into the *communication strategy*.
» Then goals have to be set for each element of the communication mix (see Chapter 2), leading to strategies for each.
» Finally there have to be *tactics* for each element of the promotional mix.

Strategy should always be based as much as possible on *facts*, as these are usually more reliable than pure hunches. While there are still people who have that gut feeling and can be successful, the fact is that this number is very small, in spite of the fact that they do attract attention when their hunch plays off! Here is a simple timeline (Fig. 6.1) that can be used to set the strategic and tactical aims for a brand, and the type of promotional intention, during the life cycle of a product.

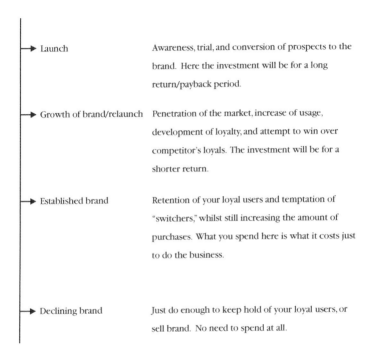

Launch — Awareness, trial, and conversion of prospects to the brand. Here the investment will be for a long return/payback period.

Growth of brand/relaunch — Penetration of the market, increase of usage, development of loyalty, and attempt to win over competitor's loyals. The investment will be for a shorter return.

Established brand — Retention of your loyal users and temptation of "switchers," whilst still increasing the amount of purchases. What you spend here is what it costs just to do the business.

Declining brand — Just do enough to keep hold of your loyal users, or sell brand. No need to spend at all.

Fig. 6.1 A timeline charting sales promotional strategy over the life cycle of a product.

Never waste time or budget on promoting brands that are in terminal decline; you might just as well "milk" them while they may yet have some payback. And don't bother with small-scale, ineffective promotions as all that happens is that the benefits of those that are really important are watered down and the cost of waste is increased. Additionally, they can be an irritant to the buyers of your more vital brands.

Now is a good time to check on the classification of the promotion mechanics, since much has already been mentioned about one type of scheme and another. Basically there are only four factors which can be brought into play when deciding how to formulate a promotion.

1 Do you add value?
2 Do you give money off (the price)? (Remember price is the only source of revenue.)
3 Do you add value instantly or in a delayed fashion?
4 Do you give money off instantly or in a delayed fashion?

Table 6.1 below sets out the options and how best they should be used.

Table 6.1   Promotional options represented in terms of timing.

Type of promotion	Instant	Delayed
Value promotion	Free in-pack offer	Free mail-in
	Reusable container	Competition
	Instant win	Self-liquidating premium
	Home sampling	Charity-type promotion
	Free on-pack item	
Price promotion	Pence-off flash	Next-purchase coupon
	Buy one, get one free	Cash refund
	Extra product	Cash share-out
	In-store coupon	Buy-back deal
	Finance offer	

Management then has to assess the use of each of these mechanics when set against the reason for the sales promotion. This can be done by creating a grid with the objectives along one axis and the mechanics along the other, and then grading them as to their application. For example, to increase volume you would use immediate free offers or immediate price offers and grant, say, nine points.

Having established the need and objectives for the sales promotion, top management must then stand four-square behind it and approve the scheme before it goes any further and incurs charges. This means budget approval, legal clearance, and any other form of inter-company rules that have to be adhered to. This means that responsibility is accepted at the highest level and does not repose on a junior- or middle-ranking executive who could bring disaster down on the company without the board knowing, as was the case with the ill-fated Hoover promotion, the effects of which are still being felt. The promotion offered two free flights to the US for £100 or more spent on any Hoover product. The take-up was phenomenal. The catch was in the small print, which stated that participants had to book accommodation, car hire, and insurance to the value of at least £300. However, the company grossly underestimated the redemption level and many people could not even get their flights because of inadequate management and poor handling of the whole scheme. Additionally, people asked how was it possible for two free flights to be funded out of the profits from the sale of an appliance.

The management of Hoover resigned as a result and the whole sales promotion industry was called into question, with doubts being raised in the House of Commons. Many people took the company to court and the owners reserved £20mn to try to put the matter right. This is now a textbook case history which serves to reinforce the notion that it is vital that everyone in the organization fully knows and understands the implications of running a sales promotion scheme, and demonstrates the potential there is for a company's reputation to be destroyed in a moment of stupidity or through the lack of total quality planning.

Proper briefing concerning promotions has to be carried in good time out to ensure that the buying department has sufficient stocks for manufacture and that there is a sufficient inventory to meet demand. Transport and distribution need to know, as they are likely to have to deliver more stock, and of course the sales force personnel have to be thoroughly briefed as they are the front-line troops. Other departments involved will be the advertising and public relations departments, as they will inherently be involved in any event, and the sales office staff handling the detail. Often overlooked are the telephonists, who need to know what is going on as they are usually the first people to be spoken to by members of the public or trade. It all boils down to good internal communications. But first and foremost comes the top management, who must sign off and give the go-ahead to any promotion.

BUDGET

One of the most important aspects of any promotion is the amount of money allocated to it, or to the whole program of promotions on an annual basis; here the accountant will be involved as keeper of the corporate purse. How is the budget arrived at and on what basis is a decision finally taken? Eventually, of course, top management must give its approval, based on properly thought through reasoning.

Historically, many businesses have merely taken last year's spend and provided a little extra to account for rising costs and inflation. Others have taken a fixed percentage of their revenue or turnover, based on past tradition or the accepted norm for the industry. Yet others seem to think that by spending in line with, or in ratio to, competitors they will be near enough the right level. Then there are the more enlightened organizations who decide how much will really need to be spent to achieve the clearly defined overall marketing objectives. This latter method is regarded as being the right way, since the others take little or no account of the ability to fund the agreed promotion program and absolutely no account of what the market is doing or the company's own ambitions in it.

TIMING

A further top management decision will need to be taken as to the timing of promotions, as they could seriously interfere with other major corporate activity being planned around the same times. Decide:

» when the promotion is best going to impact on the target audience;
» how long it should run for, depending on the type of promotion you are organizing; and
» what lead time is needed to brief everyone (as above) and get delivery of all print, prizes, supporting materials, etc.

(Note: Experience shows that far more time needs to be allotted to setting up and organizing promotions than is expected. Rule: Always build in a time safety factor to allow for errors, delays, and problems.)

COMMUNICATION

Often overlooked, or poorly handled by top management who should oversee all the final detail, is the vital communication element, i.e. how the promotion is to be merchandised/promoted/advertised to its targeted market. This involves:

» product wrappers;
» printed material in or on the pack/product;
» individual leaflets (including racks);
» media advertising (now very common) to help the promotion get off the ground – many advertisements carry promotions as their main function and, in today's fast-moving world, a Website will help to secure high visibility;
» sales aids for representatives;
» direct mail in support of the promotion; and
» posters and stickers (even a new postal franking stamp).

It is important, when spending so much time, money, and effort, that you get as "big a bang for your bucks" as possible, and that is why every sensible opportunity must be seized to ensure that what you are doing is talked about as much as possible.

LEGAL MATTERS

It has already been shown how damaging a promotion can be if it is not properly thought out, and how your company could end up in the courts for failing to deliver the offer, even when it is made in good faith. There is a real need, therefore, for companies to realize that there is a British Code of Sales Promotion Practice, which is a self-regulatory code written by people in the sales promotion business in their own long-term interests. The premise is that it is better for the industry to self-regulate than to have laws imposed upon it. It is supported by the Code of Advertising Practice (CAP) and comes under the supervision of the Advertising Standards Authority (ASA). Other countries also have codes, e.g. Malaysia and Singapore, but many are based on the UK's code.

Although this code is not a substitute for the legal protection of the public, producer, or distributor against fraudulent practice, it does complement the law. As there are many laws governing lotteries, prize draws, and so-called games of chance, which appear regularly in sales promotions, it well behoves senior management to ensure that their promotion will not contravene any aspect of the code or laws. (There are in fact more than a hundred British laws that affect the way sales promotions are conducted and now there are many EU Directives too.) This means that every care must be taken to ensure that only those promotions that are to be mounted are cleared before they are let loose either in this country or abroad. If this means getting legal advice, then accept the charges and build them into the costs of the promotion. These costs will be far less than the costs of being told to withdraw an already expensive promotion scheme.

The British sales promotion industry has an enviable reputation for being supremely creative and honest. However, there are always threats from the EU to make changes which could seriously harm not just the business in the UK but also that in other member states, which could deny millions of people of the innocent pleasure they derive from participating in simple fun and which brightens up their days. The UK's Institute of Sales Promotion is the body that could initially advise organizations unsure of where to turn for help. There are some fundamental requirements that every promoter must observe, if they wish to avoid being taken to task over a slackly thought-out scheme. Promotions should be:

» legal, decent, honest, and truthful;
» conducted equitably, promptly, and efficiently;
» seen to deal fairly and honorably with consumers;
» in line with accepted principles of fair competition;
» unlikely to bring the industry into disrepute (see Hoover above); and
» in accordance with the spirit, as well as the letter, of the rules.

Management must take all this into account and, with the various changes that are being made, keep their house clean, in order to ensure that governments (national, European, and otherwise) do not feel justified in imposing their own controls, which many fear could be draconian. And yet there are instances where promotions, run by those who should really know better, are censured by the ASA in the UK for failing one or other of these tenets.

As can be seen from this list, organizing and implementing any promotion cannot be left to a relative junior as it was at one time, when promotional activity was often regarded as the poor relation to mainstream or above-the-line advertising. The sheer sums of money now allocated to promotions and the sophisticated marketing planning of which promotion now forms a part require that, at the very least, top management understands the value, and the potential danger, of this marketing tool in the overall corporate strategy.

USING OUTSIDE SUPPLIERS

There is no one organization in existence that can satisfy all its promotional requirements in-house. It is important, then, to know who to turn to, so as to ensure that all aspects of your promotion are handled correctly, on time, and at the contracted price. Since very rarely are two promotions alike, it is common to find different sets of suppliers being contracted, as many of them have specialist skills. The real skill of finding the right supplier is to work with them for as much of the time as possible, in order that a long-term relationship can be developed. The alternative is to send out specifications to a number of suppliers and to decide whom to use, based on price, terms, and perhaps reputation.

There are some organizations in both the public and private sector that require at least three separate quotations for everything that will be needed. This can reach the heights of stupidity when, as happened with the author, a company in question tried to get quotations from other suppliers for an item that was patented and only available from the one source.

Sales promotion agencies

While smaller companies try to manage promotions in-house, very few who organize them have much detailed knowledge of the subtle art of promotion. In larger organizations they may well come under the control of a sales promotion manager, who may then have to work with non-specialist colleagues. It is no wonder then that the most successful and most talked-about schemes are designed and, in many cases, implemented by sales promotion agencies, often referred to as "consultancies" as much of their income is derived from fees rather than from commission, although they do "sell" artwork and many other services. The term "agency" is usually applied to firms providing a wide range of marketing/advertising services. As in advertising, many agencies tend to specialize in certain industries or product groupings such as consumer goods, although a really professional agency should be able to tackle most products and services. They all have a number of similar features.

» They charge for original concepts and ideas on a fee basis. This means that the client, if they so wish, can worry about all the implementation of a promotion.
» Promotion agencies can provide a wide range of ancillary services, from finished artwork to handling competition entries and sending out prizes.
» Many agencies are available on an ad hoc basis and are paid retainers, or they work on an ongoing basis, which is probably better for both parties.
» As many executives in sales promotion agencies have a wide knowledge of all the necessary requirements for organizing a successful promotion, it makes sense to use a "one-stop shop" where advice will be unbiased and enthusiasm high, especially amongst the smaller or newer ones which are anxious to make their mark.

How do you find the right agency?

The Sales Promotion Consultants Association (see Chapter 9 for contact details) will help put together a folio of work from a number of suitable agencies for clients to view, and a number of specialist journals highlight or feature the work of many in the promotions world. Recommendation is valuable but not infallible. Much will depend on the chemistry of those who will be working together, the location of the agency, and the methods of communication needed to ensure quick agreement on a whole range of activities. The client should prepare a thorough brief and invite a maximum of three agencies to pitch. A decision should be taken as soon as is feasible and the losers told why they failed to win the business.

What to look for in an agency

» Top of the list has to be creativity – this is what you are really buying into. Fresh and innovative thinking is at a premium and for this you should be prepared to pay.
» Excellent communication skills – they should not be in the business if they haven't mastered this art.
» Firm financial control – it's your money they will be spending, after all.
» Great service – keeping customers happy means that they will keep customers.
» A track record of success – if they have one. Ask other clients what they think, and enquire of the editors of the trade press such as *Incentive Today* and *Sales Promotion* (see Chapter 9 for contact details). They have their fingers on the promotion industry's pulse and could guide you in your search for the most suitable agency.

A point that will always crop up is the payment of a fee to the pitching agencies for their involvement thus far. Some smaller agencies will be glad to do the work for nothing if they feel there is a good chance of winning the business, whereas other agencies will expect some fee in recognition of their professionalism. When a decision has been reached as to the selected agency, make sure that you and your staff get to know the agency team who will be working closely with your business. A better team spirit will then work in your favour and you will get more out of the agency as a result. But never expect an agency to do much more than what it is contracted to do without paying extra fees.

Field marketing agencies

There are times when, to gain extra rapid coverage of the outlets you normally deal with, you need to have extra staff to assist – maybe to get the promotion out into these outlets faster than your own sales people could. This is when the field marketing agencies play such an important role. Their personnel can be an extension to your own full-time staff on a permanent basis, or they can be used on a project basis according to needs. The people employed by agencies are part-time but can be used to fulfil many sales-type functions, such as placing display material, selling, giving out samples and leaflets, and so on. Their use during promotional periods can play a decisive part in the success or otherwise of the event.

A good agency can act as an extension to your own operation, providing much more than just people. For example, they will plan journey cycles, monitor and analyze results, and keep their team equipped with all the items that they need to do the job contracted. The author has worked with a number of field marketing agencies and has found the staff employed by them to be very professional. Of course, they do need to be fully briefed and properly equipped, but they also need to be carefully selected for the type of outlets they will be working in and the type of products they will be selling or promoting, because they are ambassadors for your company and must reflect its values and image while "on duty". Regarding the rates charged, you will have to negotiate with the agency a rate per call or for the overall campaign, and this will depend on many factors such as travel, reporting systems, and the type of work involved. Check also who will design and produce the special costumes that may be required in some promotions.

Handling houses

Once a promotion has been set up and is about to roll, it is a bit late in the day to wonder how to cope with all the entry forms, premium offers, and money, along with all the computerization of collected data and a myriad other day-to-day aspects which have to be attended to so that the promotion runs smoothly and avoids creating problems with your most precious asset – your customers. It makes sense, therefore, to farm out all these functions to a handling house, which will then relieve your company of the responsibility, for a fee. The Response Council (see Chapter 9) has a checklist that should be discussed to ensure that nothing is overlooked in the brief given and taken. The checklist covers:

» the nature of the promotion;
» the handling needs – e.g. goods, money, coupons, and entry forms;

» timing – when and for how long the promotion is scheduled;
» anticipated response to the scheme;
» how the promotion is featured – e.g. on pack or by direct mail;
» response format – e.g. coupons, labels, or advertisement cut-outs;
» handling cash, cheques, security of credit cards, and the setting-up of a special bank account;
» despatch procedures – e.g. van, post, and costs;
» system for packing and the standard necessary to ensure safe arrival at destination;
» storage of items and their security, taking into account any special considerations – e.g. inward stock-counting and checking for quality/breakage;
» insurance of both parties;
» how much data is to be captured and on what system;
» requirements for regular reports and updates – e.g. audits on stock and other data; and
» stock control, reorder levels, who is to place the top-up order, and the disposal of unused stock.

These are the main issues that should be clarified if you are to avoid future wrangling over what was expected of whom. Advice: Treat the handling house as a close ally and build a good working relationship with them over a period of time. Visit their premises, check all the facilities, ensure the working systems are in place, and meet the staff to discover how well they have been trained and to satisfy yourself that they are really competent. By using the same means as were used to locate a sales promotion agency, it is possible to select a handling house you will be comfortable working with.

Point-of-purchase suppliers and specialist printers

There can be few outlets of any type that do not have some form of point-of-purchase (POP) material – once known and sold by the author as point-of-sale material, but today renamed to avoid confusion with EPOS (electronic point of sale). Even the humble leaflet dispenser has a vital role to play, not only in luring customers and prospects into taking a leaflet, but also in carrying the brand's values and image with it in the most relevant way. The fact that there are so many diverse types of material drawing attention, or promoting special deals and offers, is indicative of the power of the medium even in today's high-tech world. The use of light, movement, and sound coupled with computerized displays allows promoters to become ever more innovative in their ways of capturing shoppers' attention and action. Long gone are the days when display material consisted of a dump bin and a few shelf-talkers with maybe a light-powered moving image. Interactive units are now on the scene in the new shopping malls, and anywhere people gather and can be sold to.

Before briefing a POP company, decide just what will be the function and purpose of the display and where it will be situated in the venue it will be installed in. Try to encompass the theme of your advertising strategy and promotional concept in the display, so that all aspects of the campaign are enhanced. If this means that you can use the most modern computer-generated graphics, then never hesitate to use state-of-the-art techniques. Finally, check on the maintenance of the equipment. Can it be subcontracted? Can you expect to sell expensive POP equipment to retailers for their use or would the retailer charge you for the retail space it occupies?

Should your promotion involve an instant-win promotion, scratch cards, or games, it is imperative that the correct number of tickets and so on are printed and that none are leaked, counterfeited, or improperly distributed. This is when the average jobbing printer can find himself out of his depth, for the range of security devices now being used to prevent fraud is extensive and expensive. From special inks to ultraviolet light, holograms, and three-dimensional technology, security printers have a vast array of anti-fraud ploys available to defeat even the wiliest, many of which remain secret even from their clients. Just to be extra safe, check out their own security arrangements and whether they carry insurance that specifically covers the type of promotional print that you are going to use. On the subject of insurance for promotions, it is worth knowing how you can cover against certain eventualities and what it entails.

Insurance for promotions

What happens if the promotion is so successful that it wrecks your budget? What happens if you have to cancel the whole promotion? What happens if, in spite of all the checking, there is a printer's error resulting in more than the number of winners allowed for? And do you need cover for all the ancillary events that could surround a promotion? The simple answer is that you can take out insurance against these sorts of disasters. There is a specialist insurer in the UK called PIMS (see Chapter 9 for contact details), who will calculate the expected redemption rate and advise on the amount of cover and the necessary premium. The benefits are that promoters will sleep easily in the knowledge that if something is to go wrong it inevitably will go wrong, but they will still have a job. The cost of the cover is a true business cost. Advice: Never leave this aspect of a promotion to the last minute; indeed, involve the insurer fairly early on in the development of the promotion, so that they can more accurately assess the risks and maybe advise on some of the riskier elements of it which may have escaped you or your agency.

THE FUTURE

There will always be "sales promotions" of whatever type. What has to be recognized is that the shape and speed of the technical media have brought in their train yet another method by which promoters and participants alike can communicate with one another. Now that the Internet, the World Wide Web, and other gizmos have shrunk the world still further, fresh opportunities will open up to those bold and brave enough to seize them and to design schemes to fit the medium. At the same time everyone must be careful not to create situations that could give rise to controls or restrictions being imposed by governments, not all of which have the same "free" trading views as others.

NOTES

1 Brown, C. (1993) *The Sales Promotion Handbook*. Kogan Page, London.
2 Ehrenberg, A., Hammond, K., and Goodhardt, C.A.E. (1991) "The after-effects of consumer promotions." The London Business School Centre for Marketing and Communications.

Sales Promotion in Practice

» Tips on making sales promotion schemes better.
» Award schemes and the 2001 prizewinner (UK).
» Multiple-client promotion.

Sales promotion campaigns are some of the most useful, flexible, creative, and cost-effective ways of winning and keeping business. However, all promoters must remember one of the great fundamentals of any business, and that is that "trial" is temporary. Repurchase depends on the product/service quality. Cynics label sales promotion as nothing more than a "bribe," but of course they fail totally to appreciate the rigors of competition in the real world. The result of a sales promotion should be satisfied customer needs, as well as some harmless extra enjoyment for the entrant/participant in making the transaction. Promoters should also realize that it is easier for a promotion to have a negative rather than a positive effect on the company's image, as has already been illustrated with the Hoover debacle (see Chapter 6).

Here are some tips on helping to create a better sales promotion, apart from the central theme or idea.

» Promotional copy has very little time to register with a prospect or customer. Make it very clear what the offer is, and make the headline short and precise with the benefits clearly spelled out.
» Make it clear on how to take part – is it easily understandable?
» Detailed wording should be relevant to the brand and target audience.
» Avoid unnecessary adjectives and adverbs. Edit copy hard and then go back and edit again.
» Get administrative details out of the way of the basic message.
» Make the whole package interesting and be enthusiastic – create a sense of urgency (the "now" factor!).
» Ensure brand recognition is high, and use logos and relevant colours. (Logos have better recall than names.)
» Use photographs – they are easier to accept visually.
» Keep typefaces to a minimum and don't make the execution too busy/cluttered. Avoid using reversed-out colours in the print. Also avoid the use of too much upper-case type. Lower-case lettering is easier to read.
» If you are showing new/low prices against normal prices, then show the savings – which is what buyers want to know – as well as what the item will actually cost. You really want to attract buyers, not just entrants!
» People are loyal to brands not products. Repeat-buying alone is not loyalty. Loyalty is a desire to repeat. Repeat behavior can be bought,

but loyalty must be earned. Customers are an asset. Keep them happy and you'll keep them.

» Never forget that it takes more than buyers to make a successful promotion. Plan to reward your sales team, distributors, and stockists via incentives against targets, and make sure everyone in the business is aware of what is going on.

» When thinking of a prize structure, never be afraid to be daring or even outrageous, as these are the types of promotions that hit the public's imagination and get talked about. Examples might include a flight in a hot air balloon; a flight in a MiG jet in Russia; a hair cut in New York; shopping at Harrods – any time – and selecting up to £1000 of goods; winning 200 hours of skiing in Aspen, Colorado; winning 200km of videotape (how many videotapes this represents is too hard to calculate, but it sounds an awful lot!). Equally, the prize slogan "Win a Vineyard for a Year" has a certain ring to it, and how can it be properly evaluated?

» Express the prizes in large figures – they will convey a much stronger message. For example "Win 200 Hours of Skiing" sounds far more exciting than "Win a Holiday in Aspen." Some years ago the Co-op in the UK ran a "£1 Million Price Cut" promotion, which was more impactful than a few pence off this and that. A new car launch included 1000 miles of free motoring (i.e. gasoline) which sounded rather better than the equivalent cost of the gasoline.

The UK has for many years been regarded as one of the world's leading practitioners in sales promotion design, creativity, and use in its overall marketing mix. This is due partly to the greater freedom to run such a wide variety of promotional activity compared to many other parts of the world, where it is seen as giving one company an unfair advantage over another, so tight restrictions as to what is allowed are imposed. But no one can doubt that over the past decade the standard of promotions has improved dramatically, as those who enter the business now undergo proper training in all aspects of this activity, organized by the Institute of Sales Promotion. Each year the ISP awards recognize the skills and talents of those operating in the UK. The Grand Prix winner is sponsored by the trade journal *Promotions and Incentives*. The latest awards for 2001 recorded nearly 500 entries, a 20% increase on the previous year, which reflects well on the importance of this marketing tool in today's business environment. What is interesting to note is the big increase in mainstream areas of event marketing, cause-related promotions, and business-to-business activity. The new e-media categories attracted 10% of the entries, showing that the medium was being used effectively and relevantly. There are now 24 individual categories, ranging from consumer and cause-related promotions to digital media promotions. This does really reflect the nature and growth of sales promotion in everyday life.

CASE STUDY 1: THE BRITISH ARMY

The Grand Prix award for 2001 went to the British Army. Traditionally, the Army advertised in January each year for recruits aged between 16 and 26. It used television to reach its target audience, which attracted sufficient numbers to make this choice of medium worthwhile. However, in recent years this approach has resulted in fewer applications, as the Army has been regarded as less and less of a career option for this age group. This, combined with increased time charges for television commercials, meant that it was becoming a less than efficient and effective advertising medium. This was the nub of the problem faced by those responsible for recruitment – how to replicate the normal level of brochure requests and visits to recruitment offices, and to build face-to-face contact between the public and Army personnel, by using an alternative promotional vehicle to achieve targets. The target was to recruit 15,000 new soldiers.

The hook was "Win Seven Nights in Kenya." The use of a competition in sales promotion as a "mechanic" or method is hardly the most innovative technique as many cynics might say but, as has been illustrated earlier, it is how the idea is treated and how unusual is the benefit on offer that makes an ordinary promotion into an outstanding one. Soldiers handed out the "Operation Kenya" competition entry cards, while magazine inserts and press and radio advertisements explained how to get involved. This media support was vital to communicate the promotion and shows the importance of a totally integrated approach to solving the problem.

The competition rules focused on attitude rather than intellect, and the reward was seven nights' training with the Army in Kenya, a really attractive, exciting, and wholly relevant prize. In days gone by, the

Navy press gangs may have been successful in their recruitment, but their methods offered very little in the way of benefits or incentives! The Army's "Seven Nights in Kenya" was simple in its message, and outstandingly well executed. The comment from Edwin Mutton, chairman of awards, was, "It proves that a competition as targeted as a rifle, as subtle as a tank and which promotes loyalty (literally) can be done with outstanding effect."

KEY INSIGHTS

This promotion succeeded on several fronts.

» It was cost-efficient.
» It hit the right audience.
» It was run at the right time of the year.
» It was different.
» It was well able to be supported in other media.

Lessons

» Understand clearly the nature of the problem you are facing – a shortfall in recruiting levels and increasing advertising costs.
» Target the market carefully – age, sex, location.
» Decide the best and most efficient type of promotion that will interest that group.
» Create an exciting and relevant theme.
» Support the promotion with other media.
» Make enough budget available to do the job.
» Evaluate the results – in this case the number of applicants and the number of recruits actually enlisted.
» Decide whether a similar scheme could be run once more.

CASE STUDY 2: THE DAILY EXPRESS *et al.*

Here is an example of a joint promotion, which involved no less than five organizations. And the only cost to those organizations was that of the prizes, which they agreed to fund. While the promotion admittedly took place many years ago, when the Marina motor car was launched in the UK, the way it was handled is still regarded as a textbook exercise in joined-up promotion. The organizations involved were the *Daily Express*, British Leyland, Castrol, Triplex (heated rear windows), and Pirelli (tires). All were clients of a large advertising agency, Dorland, and its sales promotion division, Westbourne Promotions.

The Marina was to be launched in the media, using press, television, and cinema. There were the usual roadshows and exhibitions to lend it support. The *Daily Express* was on the media schedule, so the promotions department approached them with a view to running an exclusive competition where the main prize would be the first car off the production lines. The other clients were then approached to see whether they would be interested in joining in a motoring-theme promotion/competition and making their products available as runner-up prizes. The *Daily Express* carried the competition for three weeks in a prominent position, charging only six old pence per entry. Multiple entries were encouraged. In addition, the day before the real launch, the paper carried a teaser earpiece, showing the car in silhouette form, advising readers that they could win this new car and loads of other motoring-related prizes. In effect, the car got a head start in its own launch program.

The competition was simplicity itself. Readers were given 10 important features of the new car and had to place them in an order that they thought was the most important, and then complete a tiebreak sentence/phrase. The sequence that matched the judges' was the winner.

KEY INSIGHTS

» The *Daily Express* was always looking for an idea to attract readers and was well known for organizing exciting promotions to retain and attract them. Competitions using cars are sure-fire winners and, as this was a new design, they wanted to give it all the promotional firepower at its disposal.

» By charging a modest sixpence for each entry, the *Daily Express* soon recouped any costs incurred, including the cost of the car which they did buy on favourable terms!

» The cost of the space the *Daily Express* gave over to the promotion was their own cost.
» The amount of free coverage all the other companies received for the cost of their own prizes was immense and everyone gained from the exposure over the three weeks.
» The *Daily Express* seized the opportunity to capitalize on the back of someone else's product to attract more readers, which in turn worked for all the participants, who promoted their involvement through their own outlets. It was almost like squaring the circle.

CASE STUDY 3: AUTOBYTEL.COM

Here is a promotion, run in the US, which used the electronic media as a vehicle for communicating with its target audience. The promoter is Autobytel.com, which organized through its agency "The 4-Door To Your Door" instant win game. The target audience was PC owners in the market to purchase a car or car-related services within the next 12 months.

The objectives were:

» to drive online and offline users to the site, and help them understand the value of Autobytel as the primary online resource for buying a car;
» to educate users about Autobytel's service and how to use it;
» to capture data from new and existing members; and
» to surpass the 2% industry click-through rates for direct marketing e-mails.

A "Match and Win" instant game required players to match their "car key" (distributed both online and offline) with the key featured on the Autobytel site. Car keys were distributed online via promotional banner advertisements and direct mail e-mail campaigns, and offline via newspaper overwraps. A "second chance" drawing gave non-winners another opportunity to win a prize. Prizes were a new car, computers, free pizzas, and cinema tickets.

The results were quite remarkable.

» Some 3 million people hit the registration page.
» Response to the mailings was extraordinarily high, ranging from 5% to 45%.
» Over 200,000 unique registrations were received.

The highly targeted online/offline direct marketing effort focused on consumers who had expressed interest in buying a car, and consumer interest was heightened by targeted and timely messages that were both interactive and amusing. The results showed that clever use of "new" media can produce good leads and business. (Note: This promotion was created for Autobytel.com by Promotions.com and can be located on their Website at www.promotions.com.)

KEY INSIGHTS

» This was a superb example of a promotion geared to PC users, but targeting likely car buyers through the "new" medium.
» The campaign helped build a follow-up mailing list, so vital in making the promotion even more efficient and cost-effective.
» The prizes and their spread were cleverly chosen and relevant, giving non-main prizewinners something as well. Good public relations work ensured wide media coverage and exposure.
» The mechanics (i.e. what entrants had to do) were kept simple and the rewards were almost instant.

CASE STUDY 4: PEPSI

Here is an example of a very simple but highly successful promotion that was run in the Indian city of Bangalore back in 1990 by Pepsi, who decided to test-market their product there. The company placed an advertisement in the local newspaper which invited readers, who were impressed by what it had told them about Pepsi, to tear out the advertisement and take it to any soft-drinks shop where it would be exchanged for a full-size bottle of Pepsi, free!

The payback was that over 50% of the advertisements were redeemed in this manner, during the two days that the scheme ran. It generated instant sampling of the brand. The fact that no voucher had to be carefully cut out, so making it easier for those to redeem their advertisement, helped. No one was asked for a name, no money was called for, and everything was kept beautifully simple, with the retailer only having to hand over all the collected advertisements to the local Pepsi salesman for reimbursement, plus a handling allowance.

The advertisement was most attractive, with the headline "Come on Bangalore! Taste the Magic Free Today." Moreover, it was targeted to just the one city and the offer was only available for two days, making the whole promotion doubly special and urgent. This paved the way for Pepsi to become a regular soft-drinks purchase and to build a degree of loyalty.

KEY INSIGHTS

Pepsi benefited by:

» using a highly targeted market area;
» running a market test for a world-recognized brand;
» choosing a local newspaper as the vehicle to carry the promotional message;
» giving simple redemption instructions with a generous offer;
» specifying a tight promotion period to heighten the urgency factor; and
» securing the retailers' co-operation instantly.

Key Promotional Concepts and Thinkers

» Glossary of terms.
» Creativity.
» Using the media.
» Research and evaluation.
» Major thinkers.

A GLOSSARY OF SALES PROMOTION

Above the line – Used to describe any paid form of advertising, such as TV, press, cinema, or posters, on which an agency receives commission from the media. (Agencies were originally merely the sales organizations selling the media's space and it was only later that "clients" asked the agents what they should put in the space they had just bought.)

Advertising – Any form of paid-for media used by an organization to communicate with its target audience.

Advertising agency – A company that develops and implements advertising activity. Some agencies specialize in products or industries, some offer restricted services such as creative and media buying only, while others offer full services including research, sales promotion, etc.

Advertising strategy – A statement of the broad goals that the advertising is designed to achieve.

Attention – The process of arousing the interest of an individual in some desired activity.

Attitude – This word sums up the knowledge and feelings, both positive and negative, towards a subject.

Awareness – The stimulation of knowledge about a person or object.

Banded pack – A pack consisting of two (or more) of the same products, or two (or more) complementary products, banded together and offered at a special price. Confectionery and drinks are the two most common products banded together.

Below the line – Used to describe all those marketing communication activities that do not carry any commission paid to an advertising agency.

Bonus – Usually this is an extra reward offered to the trade in the form of a discount or extra free stock (a baker's dozen) in exchange for a promotional order.

Bonus pack – A pack that offers a purchaser additional volume at no extra cost.

Bounce-back – An offer to a promotional respondent, usually sent with the response package to gain extra mileage from the original promotion. (Akin to having the start of a mailing list.)

Brand – A name, term, design, symbol, or any other distinguishing feature that gives a product special and recognizable identification, and differentiates it from its competition.

Brand image – So hard to build, so easy to destroy, this is the total impression left in the customer's mind by a brand and all its associations, both functional and non-functional.

Brand switcher – The bane of manufacturers, this is the shopper who shows no loyalty to any one brand or manufacturer, and regularly switches from one to another. To be fair, when a product is no more than a commodity, such as salt or sugar, there is little that can be done to prevent switching, unless there is ongoing sales promotion activity to try to keep shoppers loyal.

Business gift – A gift presented by a company to a dealer as a token of goodwill and as a bribe to get them to take in more stock. Also known as **Dealer loader**.

Buy-back – More or less self-explanatory, as it means that there will be a refund offer where the product can be sold back to the supplier at a later date.

Charity promotion – Sometimes referred to as "cause-related marketing," this is where commercial enterprises pledge to support a charity via a levy on each product sold, however calculated, or by agreeing an amount overall. Care must be taken that the right charity is selected for your product/brand.

Competition – A sales promotion technique whereby a prize is allocated according to merit. Success is dependent upon a substantial degree of skill and/or judgement having to be exercised in solving a puzzle of some type.

Co-operative advertising – A program in which the manufacturer pays an agreed amount of the retailer's advertising costs in return for the featuring of the manufacturer's brand.

Corporate image – The way in which a company is perceived, based on its history, background, beliefs, and style of doing business.

Coupon – A voucher exchanged for a cost reduction against goods or services. It is sometimes used, confusingly, to describe an application or order form.

Creative credit – The use of changing credit terms, such as giving more credit or extending the credit period (or both), in order to encourage larger purchases by retailers or motivate them to stock a wider range of products.

Cross-promotion – A promotion in which two or more brands are marketed together, typically with one brand carrying an offer for the other. Often the offer is reciprocated.

Cross-referral coupon – A coupon given to the buyer of one product for redemption against another product, as part of a cross-promotion.

Dealer loader – Another term for **Business gift**.

Direct mail – The use of postal and other delivery techniques to communicate with a carefully targeted audience.

Direct marketing – Not to be confused with direct mail, this is an interactive system of marketing that uses one or more advertising media to effect a measurable response and/or transaction at any location.

Direct promotion – Any promotional activity that works through direct contact with the current or potential customer.

Direct selling – The process of achieving the sale of products or services without the use of intermediary sales channels such as wholesalers, dealers, or retailers.

Discount coupon – A coupon that entitles the user to savings on a wide range of leisure activities or services, such as eating out and film processing. The discount coupon is a useful ploy in attracting and retaining customers. Its perceived value is high, but the actual cost is low – the best promotional ratio.

Extra product – More product for your money, expressed as "25% more" or similar. This is a good ploy as the perceived value to the buyer is far more than the actual cost of the product supplied.

Extra-value pack – A pack containing extra fill free or at a special price.

Flash pack – A pack carrying a special message, usually relating to a special deal being offered by the promoter.

Free draw – A draw that allows winners to be determined purely by chance. There must not be the prerequisite of a payment or purchase to enter and all entries stand an equal opportunity of winning.

Free film scheme – A scheme in which a customer is provided with special low-cost developing and printing as well as being sent a new film with their prints. The scheme is forever popular and should self-perpetuate, making more money for the processor as well as giving the customer a good deal.

Free flight – A deal in which one flight is free when the second is paid for at the normal rate. Almost the "buy one, get one free" multibuy, except that the promotion is not instant, but a highly attractive deal for promoters, passengers, and airlines as an unsold seat is revenue lost forever.

Free mail-in – A reward given free to those who post in their entry, normally in exchange for proof of purchase.

Free-stay deal – A deal in which a promoter purchases a number of free-room vouchers from a specialist operator to be used by a customer to obtain free accommodation at a range of specified hotels. The customer pays for food and drink only, and may only be able to use the vouchers at certain times. The deal is extremely popular with all parties involved for its perceived and real values.

Full-service agency – An agency that offers a comprehensive service to clients, typically one that includes creative, account-handling, planning, and media elements. Sales promotion agencies are designated in the same way.

Game – A form of free draw or instant win. Prizes are awarded without the use of great skill or judgement being required by participants and without the demand for payment or proof of purchase to enter.

Gift with purchase – Self-explanatory in that a gift is awarded at the time and place of purchase. (A plastic flower with soap powder is a prime example.)

Handling house – A marketing services agency that sorts, packs, and/or mails promotional materials, gifts, etc.

Image – The creation of an identity for a product or service by its association with other values.

Incentive – A reward given to motivate a buyer to make a purchase, or use a product or service.

In-pack premium – A free gift included within the pack being promoted to consumers.

Instant win – A prize promotion based on the distribution of a set number of winning tickets. Participants do not have to pay or make a purchase to enter and they know instantly if they have won something.

Joint promotion – A promotion in which two or more enterprises decide that they can each benefit by co-operating with each other to create a "bigger bang for their bucks" than by going it alone. This works well when there is no direct competition, but each party shares a similar customer base.

Lottery – The distribution of prizes by chance but where the purchase of a ticket is necessary to qualify for entry. (Note: Great care must be exercised when planning competitions, prize draws, lotteries, and games of chance so that the laws governing them are not contravened.)

Loyalty – A measure of the propensity for customers to keep on buying a certain product or brand.

Loyalty scheme – A scheme designed to lock in a customer to your store/products by issuing them with a card that will record details of their purchases. In return, the customer can redeem any points they accumulate against goods in the store (a win-win situation). Not so popular as it was, but still used by many outlets to retain custom.

Mail-in – A promotion in which the participant mails in to gain fulfilment of the offer, normally a premium reward.

Malredemption – Nothing less than the fraudulent acquisition and cashing-in of coupons.

Marketing mix – The combined elements of the marketing program, including product, price, place, and promotion.

Misredemption – Not to be confused with malredemption, misredemption is where a customer uses a coupon but not for the product specified or intended, or where an offer is applied for when the conditions have not been met in full.

Money-off promotion – Another term for **Reduced price offer**.

Multibuy – A form of discount off the same item, offered by retailers and funded by the manufacturer. "Buy one, get one free" is printed as a flash on the pack or shelf. Although quick and easy to set up, the offer has no lasting loyalty-building qualities.

Multipack – A number of product units packed together to form a larger retail unit. A useful device when launching a new product as it will not only be an attractive offer, but it will also get customers used to the new product. In addition, it will keep out the opposition for a longer time than usual.

On-pack offer - A flat and relatively low-cost item, such as a CD or sachet of shampoo, that comes free with the magazine or other product to which it is attached. The offer is non-discriminatory (i.e. anyone can take it up) and is normally regarded by the promoter as the cost of doing business.

Overrider - An additional payment made to a trade customer for achieving agreed targets (value/volume).

Point of purchase (or sale) - Promotional items designed to attract attention in those places where the products are purchased. (Sometimes the display material can be an integral part of the original packaging, so serving a dual purpose.)

Premium promotion - A promotion in which a free gift is offered in order to encourage the purchase of a specific product or service. See also **On-pack offer**, **With-purchase premium**, **Free mail-in**, and **Self-liquidating premium**.

Prize promotion - A promotion in which participants are awarded a prize if chance favours them or their skill or judgement proves outstanding. See also **Competition**, **Free draw**, **Game**, **Instant win**, and **Probability promotion**.

Probability promotion - A promotion in which participants are asked to place in order a number of factors most important in an item, such as a car. The prize-winning answer is that which most closely agrees with the answer of an independent judge.

Promotion - The element of the marketing mix that includes all forms of marketing communication.

Promotional mix - The use in any combination of advertising, sales promotion, public relations, direct marketing, and personal selling to achieve set objectives.

Rebate - A technique whereby the buyer is given back a part of the purchase price. This is most commonly used with retailers who exceed their targets.

Reduced price offer - A promotion in which a customer is offered a product or service at a reduced price, as marked on the pack or brochure. Also known as **Money-off promotion**.

Reduced shelf price – A promotion in which a customer is offered a product at a reduced price, as marked on the shelf. The price cut is funded by either the retailer or the manufacturer.

Refund – Money returned to a customer after purchase in exchange for a proof of purchase.

Relationship marketing – Currently the buzz phrase which simply means getting closer to your customers by enhancing the levels of service, quality, and delivery of your company's output.

Sales promotion – The use of short-term and often tactical techniques to achieve short-term sales objectives.

Sample – A small amount of a product given to a prospect as a way of introducing them to it. Tight control of samples is vital in order to monitor results and prevent waste, costs, and fraud.

Seasonal discount – A price discount designed to move stock in off-peak seasons, shift end-of-line merchandise, and help merchants keep a good cash flow. Avoid the self-defeating practice of having seasonal discounts all year round or "closing-down" sales that last forever.

Self-liquidating premium – A premium/gift item funded by the participant, often at the same time as the primary purchase is made. The promotion should end up costing the promoter nothing or, at the least, very little if it has been properly administered.

Send-in – A promotion in which the respondent has to send in money/coupons to be able to participate.

Share-out – A promotion in which prize money is distributed amongst qualifying participants.

Sponsorship – The connection of a company/product with an event, whereby the promoter contributes to the cost of mounting the event in return for having the association with the event (e.g. Heineken and World Cup Rugby).

Store voucher – A voucher that can be exchanged for goods in certain big stores. The discount levels are very low, but used as incentives or prizes they are highly motivational as customers can use them to buy items they might not ordinarily purchase. The need for security is high as the vouchers represent money.

Sweepstake – A sales promotion technique whereby consumers are offered a chance to win a prize. Because of the need to satisfy the law, such promotions are rarely based on a purchase requirement.

Tailor-made promotion – A promotion specially designed for one specific customer, even if it is only a modification of an already existing scheme.

Tiebreaker – A technique used to determine the winner(s) in a competition where a number of correct answers have been received or are likely to be received.

Traffic-builder – A promotion designed to increase the "footfall" into an outlet.

With-purchase premium – A premium item available when a purchase is made. In years gone by, it was the plastic flower! Now, the use of this form of premium has moved into other areas, with quite high-ticket items being offered, such as a free TV with a new motor car.

MAJOR RELATED CONCEPTS

Creativity

You do not have to behave in a peculiar way to be creative. But you do need to suspend belief and really let your imagination take over. Then you need to know how to structure your creative ideas so that you end up with a winning promotional thought that can be turned into a practical and feasible operation.

A promotion must, above all, engage the imagination of the targeted audience. This means that there has to be a clear promotional objective and, once that is in place, then it is possible for all the other ingredients such as humor (be careful with humor!), fun, excitement, color, style, graphics, and of course the copy to be produced in the most appropriate way to "sell" to the customer. Earlier, the statement was made that promotions were really about changing behavior and, once the group that is to be influenced has been identified, it is possible to work out how best to appeal to it and the environment in which it is to be found. The next three questions should set the parameters within which the promotional ideas could fit.

1 Is the audience big enough, i.e. as a proportion of the total?
2 Can the promotion fit within the financial, legal, and timing restrictions?
3 Is the promotion easy for everyone involved to understand?

Above all ask yourself "Who do I want to do what?"

Some simple ways to get the creative mind into gear.

» List everything relevant to the type of people and the places they visit or use.
» Use mind maps to connect ideas and concepts.
» Have a brainstorming session with colleagues and throw nothing away until the time comes to start refining the ideas put forward.
» Think of yourself in a small town and try to create an interesting scenario involving the folk who live there, thinking of their likes, dislikes, and aspirations.
» Have a doppelgänger (an alter ego) and think what they might come up with.
» Keep everything simple and use up-to-date fashions, technology, words, graphics, and colors. If the promotion is going overseas, consider what is or might not be acceptable at this stage. Never lose sight of the objectives of the promotion and avoid the temptation to become too clever. Stick to the theme and the simplest mechanics possible.

Using the media

All sales promotions need to be communicated, otherwise they are dead in the water. As has been seen, the list of available media grows by the year with the main ones still being the press (national, regional, and local), television, and radio. Posters suffer from the fact that they cannot usually give readers time to note details. The best poster sites are perhaps those which large stores can erect next to their stores carrying promotional messages. Direct mail is the one medium that can carry a targeted offer right into the office or home of a prospect or customer, even carrying a sample of the item itself as a come-on.

Care must be taken to ensure that the right medium is used for the product or service being promoted and that the message itself is created by experts so that it brings the right response and action. For example it is unlikely that a special deal for a quality car would be advertised in a downmarket tabloid newspaper. More likely it would be offered to prospects via an individually typed letter (computer-generated) with an invitation to a private showing when the deal could be discussed in upmarket surroundings.

A further method is to use the door-to-door technique, whereby leaflets and even samples can be placed in homes that have been well selected or, alternatively, whole chunks of the country can be given blanket coverage if this is the right method for the job in question. Point of purchase is probably the last opportunity a promoter will have to reach customers and prospects with their special promotion details but, with the pressure on space in all outlets, it has to be an extremely clever or useful item to stand any chance of being used.

Research and evaluation

It is possible to research a promotion idea before rolling it out as a fait accompli to make sure that the theme, style, message, and mechanics selected are acceptable and will (or will not) work. A promotion can be launched in a test area to gauge response before going national. If the promotion is shown to be weak, it can be revised or scrapped before more money is spent. Too little research is conducted by companies and, as a result, many find themselves relying on hunches and tradition in the often mistaken belief that they have enough experience on which to judge their ideas. The children's and young people's markets are, however, the two areas where research has been used as the result of fast-changing fashions. Some big companies now pool their research and create a multi-company database that can be tapped into by non-competing brands and products.

It is seldom much good if no lessons are learned from running each promotion. Benchmarks need to be set against which results can be measured (whichever set of criteria is used) and the history of every promotion logged for future reference. Items covered should include promotional response, sales figures before and after the event, and finance details. Ask whether the promotion worked, why or why not, and what could have been done better. Was it all worth it? And what could have been done with the money that might have produced better results for the company? In other words, was a sales promotion the best option to solve what was perceived to be a marketing problem?

MAJOR THINKERS

It might seem strange that, for a topic which is so pervasive and where so much money is now being spent, there are not more leading lights than there are in the sales promotion industry. To be sure, there are the regular trade publications which cover events, awards, and successes in sales promotion campaigns. And there is no shortage of practitioners who eagerly beaver away on behalf of their clients or who are based in-house, many of whom have an occasional article published. There are regular conferences held, where issues both current and prospective are discussed and debated, and the Institute of Sales Promotion in the UK runs professional examinations and courses, and gives out information and advice to members.

In spite of all this, though, there is only a handful of people who could warrant having the label "major thinker" placed on their lapel. In part, this is due to the fast-changing pace of commercial life and the fact that practitioners are just getting on with their jobs. Nevertheless, a number of people have come to the fore and have had their thoughts on sales promotion published, which has helped the industry to become far more professional over the last decade or so. Many general or business writers on marketing topics tend to treat sales promotion as worth only a mention or a small chapter in the wider scope of their books. Only in more recent years has this situation begun to be reversed.

The list of people who have probably done most for the industry must include Christian Petersen, Alan Toop, Julian Cummins, John Williams, and John Wilmshurst, all of whom have been published. Writing from first-hand experience these original thinkers, apart from university lecturers, have laid down the ground rules for every practitioner or would-be practitioner to follow (see Chapter 9 for details of their books). The message that they all convey is that a sales promotion executive today has to have a number of important skills and should be suitably qualified. Although the basic theory of sales promotion may not have changed, the techniques, laws, financial controls, and systems have, meaning that those wanting to succeed now have to be multi-skilled, a far cry from the days when someone said, "Let's have a promotion!" After which, a promotion was duly pitched into the marketplace in the vague hope that it would make something happen.

One area that has attracted more "new" thinkers and thinking is that of the Internet. As this is still a relatively new medium for sales promotion, it has spawned a number of articles and even journals, for example *Promo Magazine* in the US, although even this is not exclusively given over to this medium. Many books and articles will still major on the pure advertising aspect, e.g. Neil Barrett's *Advertising on the Internet*.[1] Like many bright new ideas in days gone by, when the fax, photocopier, answerphone, etc. were all the rage, the excitement of "new" media soon passes and the latest gadgets rapidly become absorbed into our mainstream business and social life.

NOTES

1 Barrett, N. (1997) *Advertising on the Internet: How to get your message across on the World Wide Web*. Kogan Page, London.

Sales Promotion

Resources

» Trade associations and other bodies.
» Books and journals.
» EU draft legislation on a code of practice.

The sales promotion industry is particularly well represented, directly and indirectly, by a number of trade associations, agencies, and publications. While most of those listed here are UK-based, a search on the Web for items under "sales promotion" will reveal more relevant data for the country in which readers operate.

ASSOCIATIONS

The following associations are listed in alphabetical order, not by importance.

Advertising Association, Abford House, 15 Wilton Road, London SW1V 1NJ. Tel: 020 7828 2771; Fax: 020 7931 0376; Website: www.adassoc. org.uk; E-mail: aa@adassoc.org.uk

Advertising Standards Authority and Code of Advertising Practice Committee, 2 Torrington Place, London WC1E 7HW, UK. Tel: 020 7580 5555; Fax: 020 7631 3051; Website: www.asa.org.uk

Association of Promotion Marketing Agencies Worldwide (APMA Worldwide), 750 Summer Street, Stamford CT 06901, US. Tel: 203 325 3911; Fax: 203 969 1499; Website: www.apmaw.org: E-mail: mccapma@aol.com

British Promotional Merchandise Association, Bank Chambers, 15 High Street, Byfleet, Surrey KT14 7QH, UK. Tel: 01932 355660; Fax: 01932 355662: Website: www.bpma.co.uk; E-mail: enquiries@bpma.co.uk

Chartered Institute of Marketing, Moor Hall, Cookham, Maidenhead SL6 9QH, UK. Tel: 01628 427500; Website: www.cim.co.uk

European Federation of Sales Promotion, Square Vergote 34 B-1040, Brussels, Belgium. Tel: 2 735 0328

European Marketing and Promotion Association, PO Box 47, Banbury, Oxfordshire OX15 6AS, UK. Tel: 01295 678150; Fax: 01295 678155; (Secretariat) Tel: 2 230 7020; E-mail: nblow@cabinetstewart.com

Handling House, D3 Direct Ltd, Unit 8, Trident Way, International Trading Estate, Brent Way, Southall, Middlesex UB2 5LF, UK. Tel: 020 8571 6699; Fax: 020 8744 7271: E-mail: D3DirectLtd@aol.com; Contacts: David Russell/David Grad (Domestic and overseas handling house, based near Heathrow Airport.)

Institute of Sales Promotion, Arena House, 66–68 Pentonville Road, London N1 9HS, UK. Tel: 020 7837 5340; Fax: 020 7837 5326; Website: www.isp.org.uk

PIMS, Quadrant House, 80–82 Regent Street, London W1R 5PA, UK. Tel: 020 7434 3046; Fax: 020 434 0384; Website: www.pims.promo. co.uk; E-mail: ideas@pims.promo.co.uk

Point of Purchase Advertising Institute (Europe), 16 Avenue de Messine, 75008 Paris, France. Tel: 1 5375 1688; Fax: 1 5375 1688

Response Council (formerly the Promotional Handling Association and the Direct Marketing Association), 1 Oxendon Street, London SW1Y 4EE, UK.

Sales Promotion Consultants Association, 2nd Floor, 47–48 Margaret Street, London W1N 7FD, UK. Tel: 020 7580 8225; Fax: 020 7580 8189

Associations on e-business

The British Promotional Merchandise Association states that:

"Web-based promotional activity has exploded in the last two years and the internet has quickly been accepted as an essential part of any marketing campaign. However, some 50 per cent of professional marketers feel ill-equipped to harness the latest technology to their campaigns and an increasing number are handing over control of their web sites to IT professionals as a result."

This has led the UK's Chartered Institute of Marketing to form a special department, the CIM Tech International Group, to encourage greater and better use of this medium.

Specialist consultancy

Lawmark is a specialist marketing law consultancy, one of whose two principals is Philip Circus (see below for details of his book titles). Philip Circus can be reached on e-mail (philip.circus@virgin.net). The other principal is Dr Richard Lawson, author and lecturer on marketing law. Topics covered include: lotteries, games, prize competitions, promotional offers, instant wins, and "try me free" offers. Fees are charged, usually on an hourly basis.

TRADE JOURNALS IN THE UK

Incentive Today, Blenheim House, 630 Chiswick High Road, London W4 5BG, UK. Tel: 020 8742 2828; Fax: 020 8742 0329

Marketing, 174 Hammersmith Road, London W6 7JP, UK. Tel: 020 7413 4150; Fax: 020 7413 4504; Website: www.marketing.haynet.com; E-mail: 100433.2576@compuserve.com

Marketing Week, St Giles House, 50 Poland Street, London W1V 4AX, UK. Tel: 020 8439 4222; Fax: 020 8434 1439; Website: www.marketing-week.co.uk/mw0001

Promotions and Incentives, 174 Hammersmith Road, London W6 7JP, UK. Tel: 020 7413 4152; Fax: 020 7413 4509

Promotion News, Bank Chambers, 15 High Road, Byfleet, Surrey KT14 7QH, UK. Tel: 01932 355660; Fax: 01932 355662; Website: www.bpma.co.uk; E-mail: enquiries@bpma.co.uk

Sales Promotion, Market Link Publishing, The Mill, Bearwalden Business Park, Wendens Ambo, Saffron Walden, Essex CB11 4JX, UK. Tel: 01799 544200; Fax: 01799 544203

Journals on e-business

Two journals that may from time to time carry useful items about sales promotion on the Internet are:

e.business, Crimson Publishing, 14 Northfields, London SW18 1UU, UK. Website: www.ebusiness.uk.com; E-mail: ben@crimsonpublishing.co.uk

Internet Business, Haymarket Publishing, 174 Hammersmith Road, London W6 7JP, UK. Website: www.ibmag.co.uk; E-mail: Internet-Business.eds@haynet.com

BOOKS ON SALES PROMOTION AND RELATED TOPICS

Bird, D. (1993) *Commonsense Direct Marketing*, 3rd ed. Kogan Page, London.

Brown, C. (1993) *The Sales Promotion Handbook*. Kogan Page, London.

Circus. P. (1998) *Sales Promotion and Direct Marketing Law: A practical guide*, 3rd ed. Butterworths, London.

Circus, P. and Painter, T. (1989) *Sales Promotion Law*. Butterworths, London.

Cummins, J. (1998) *Sales Promotion: How to create and implement campaigns that really work*, 2nd ed. Kogan Page, London.

Petersen, C. (1994) *Sales Promotion in Action*. Gower, Aldershot.

Petersen, C. and Toop, A. (1994) *Sales Promotion in Postmodern Marketing*. Gower, Aldershot.

Petersen, C. and Ferrée, H. (eds.) (1974) *Handbook of Consumer Sales Promotion: A comprehensive and practical guide*. Kluwer-Harrap, London.

Piper, J. (ed.) (1980) *Managing Sales Promotion*. Gower, Farnborough, Hants.

Robinson, W.A. (1982) *Best Sales Promotions*. Crain Books, Chicago, IL.

Robinson, W.A. and Schultz, D.E. (1988) *Sales Promotion Management*. NTC Business Books, Lincolnwood, IL.

Robinson, W.A. and Hauri, C. (1991) *Promotional Marketing: Ideas and techniques for success in sales promotion*. NTC Business Books, Lincolnwood, IL.

Robinson, W.A. and Schultz, D.E. (1998) *Sales Promotion Essentials: The 10 basic sales promotion techniques – and how to use them*, 3rd ed. NTC Business Books, Lincolnwood, IL.

Toop, A. (1994) *Crackingjack: Sales promotion techniques*. Gower, Aldershot.

Toop, A. (1992) *European Sales Promotion: Great campaigns in action*. Kogan Page, London.

Williams, J. (1983) *The Manual of Sales Promotion*. Innovation, London.

Wilmshurst, J. (1993) *Below-the-line Promotion*. Butterworth-Heinemann, Oxford.

EU DRAFT LEGISLATION ON A CODE OF PRACTICE

Promoters in Europe should be aware of a draft document published by DG SANCO, the Directorate General for Consumer Protection and Public Health. This document sets out proposals to harmonize consumer protection across the EU and incorporates two alternatives that would introduce a minimum level of legal protection and a list of illegal practices, as well as encouraging increased co-operation between national authorities and self-regulation at the European level.

However, the DG MARKT, the Internal Market Directorate General, is expected to propose that a single market for sales promotion should be developed on the basis of the country-of-origin principle, i.e. a company running a promotion within its home country's rules should be able to run that promotion across the whole of the EU. At its most extreme, DG SANCO's initiative could mean that the country-of-destination rule is introduced, i.e. a company operating in a country other than its home base would need to operate within the rules of the destination country. This could mean that the less liberally minded countries could erect protectionist barriers, which would destroy the ethos of the single market. For more information, e-mail Nick Blow (nblow@cabinetstewart.com). Should the DG SANCO's proposals hold sway, then many generally acceptable promotional customs, schemes, and concepts would be outlawed, denying many people much harmless fun and interest in their daily purchasing lives.

Ten Steps to Making Sales Promotion Work

The 10 steps for effective sales promotion are as follows.

1 Understand or know your customers.
2 Set objectives and plan strategy.
3 Apply the basic principles of the decision-making process.
4 Understand the techniques/mechanics of promotions.
5 Do your research.
6 Set a clear reward structure.
7 Decide on an implementation plan and check it rigorously.
8 Take legal advice before running international promotions.
9 Evaluate the success of your promotion.
10 Conduct a total review.

INTRODUCTION

A great deal has been covered in presenting the wide canvas that makes up the background of sales promotion. However, putting it all together to make a successful promotion is no guarantee that it has to be, or will be, the success that is hoped for or dreamed of. What is needed is a relatively simple format that can be followed and adapted where necessary to accommodate the requirements of the promoting company. To keep it simple, 10 easy steps are highlighted which should encompass all that companies need to do – success may not be guaranteed, but at least avoidable errors won't cause any failure to be worse!

1. UNDERSTAND OR KNOW YOUR CUSTOMERS

Customers can be a fickle lot, and it is an unwise organization that claims to fully understand their customers merely because they have been buying products or services from them for many years and seem content to go on doing so. Brand leaders do not become and stay brand leaders by accident. Only by diligently researching their markets and monitoring their progress against benchmarks and the overall environment can they hope to achieve this status.

"Brand" is the sum of superb quality, great value, and an excellent image. Every organization strives to create the best image in the minds of those whose behavior and attitudes it seeks to change. Sales promotion is all about encouraging someone to try a product or service and then to remain loyal to your company or firm. Sales promotion is not, or should not be, a stand-alone activity. It should be regarded as part of the marketing mix, which includes:

» advertising
» sales promotion
» publicity
» direct selling
» direct marketing.

The proper understanding of this will help a promoter to create the right climate not just for a sales promotion but also for the overall business of communication marketing in such highly competitive times. Additionally, it must be remembered that sales promotion in particular can impact on every aspect of the marketing mix.

It has also to be understood that a sales promotion will not on its own salvage a failing product, as it is by definition a relatively short-term activity designed to achieve other objectives. At best, a sales promotion can only delay a failing product's demise. The implementation of a total quality policy within an organization will assist sales promotion thinking, planning, and implementation, as it will ensure that each item or component is thoroughly checked before any serious commitments are made. Potentially costly errors can then be avoided.

2. SET OBJECTIVES AND PLAN STRATEGY

The objective of every promotion should be that they are *SMART – specific, measurable, achievable, relevant,* and *timed*. So, before any creative time or money is invested, planners should satisfy themselves that what they are proposing is SMART. Alongside these points, the following questions need to be posed and answered truthfully, as otherwise it will be a promotion for promotion's sake.

» Where is the brand positioned in its market?
» What is the real task of the promotion? To increase volume/trial/repeat purchase/loyalty? Or to move slow-selling items, help a distributor, or merely be a nuisance to a competitor launching a new brand/product?
» Who is your target audience?
» What change do you want to make with regard to their behavior?
» Do you know what could prevent you from running the promotion selected e.g. legal issues, budget, etc.?
» Can you carry out the *measurable* part of the SMART mnemonic? Is it easy to determine the right criteria?

3. APPLY THE BASIC PRINCIPLES OF THE DECISION-MAKING PROCESS

Be creative

There is no magic formula that will turn someone into a creative genius. However, some simple guidelines could help produce a spark of an idea, which might be capable of being fanned into something exciting, different, and yet practical. For it is *the idea* that has to be worked on, as it is the be-all and end-all of a promotion. Practitioners have to understand the marketing rationale and then, using various techniques such as brainstorming, listing, and mind-mapping, decide which of the forthcoming ideas can work best. *Simple* and *relevant* are two good words to bear in mind at this stage.

Set a realistic budget

Some promoters have only a vague notion as to how a realistic budget should be arrived at. Some spend what they spent last year plus a bit allowing for inflation, while others take a fixed percentage of last year's turnover. What should be budgeted for is enough money to do the job properly. If, after serious consideration, it is felt that not enough can be allocated, then the promotion envisaged should be dropped so as not to waste any money or further effort and time.

Select the right promotion

Not always easy to determine, but very necessary, as there are so many different approaches available from which to choose and the wrong scheme could be less than satisfactory. Here, knowledge of your market, what the job of the promotion is, the type of outlet concerned, and budgetary and legal constraints will help determine how to proceed. Alongside these considerations will be what are known as "the mechanics," that is what the customer or trader is expected to do to acquire the benefit offered in the promotion. Keeping it simple, as with the creative principle above, is still a good rule.

Respect the code of practice

Never fail to have regard for the national code of practice and the various laws covering promotional schemes. Always seek the advice of a lawyer if there is any doubt as to the legality of what you are about to do. Treat the cost as part of the promotion's budget and also as good insurance.

Employ media support and outside resources

Seldom can a promotion succeed without media support, whichever kind is employed. Many promotions now enjoy TV coverage, which has the double benefit of promoting not only the promotion but also the promoting company. Others have vast coverage in the press and on the radio. To succeed, a promotion has to have the widest exposure, so it is imperative that all the media options are properly and fully explored to ensure that the right target audience has the maximum number of opportunities to see and hear about it. Additionally, if outside organizations are used, such as prize suppliers, printers, and handling houses, make sure that they come with a good track record and that you can work well with them. This includes sales promotion agencies as well. Give them all a tight brief and don't keep changing your mind, as this usually spells doom and gloom.

4. UNDERSTAND THE TECHNIQUES AND MECHANICS OF PROMOTIONS

The selection of techniques now available to promoters can be, and probably is, truly bewildering. Decisions have to be taken as to whether an offer should be instant or delayed, or should consist of cash/discount or more product for the same price as previously charged. Experience will help, of course, as to what will work best for certain products/services, but much will also depend on the image of the promoting company and how it will be perceived by the public/market at large.

Having carefully selected the correct promotion (as far as this can be ascertained), the other side of the promotion coin is to ensure that participants do not have to be budding Einsteins to appreciate what they have to do to join in, by when, and with what results. Participants should also believe that everything about the promotion is according to the code – fair, level, and above board.

Taking the two aspects together, techniques and mechanics, the watchword should then be KISS – Keep It Simple Stupid! The more complex the entry rules or instructions, the more likely a promotion will founder on the rocks of lack of interest or apathy.

5. DO YOUR RESEARCH

There are a number of ways to research a promotion before it is "rolled out" nationally or regionally. The quickest and least expensive is to organize small focus groups, who will be asked to pronounce on your suggestions and ideas (suitably masked). As long as there is a set questionnaire, then all the answers can be properly compared and some meaningful conclusions arrived at.

Another way is to run a pilot scheme in a chosen area to gauge response, but care must be taken to ensure that this area is not given undue weighting in terms of other resources used, which could produce a biased result. The benefit of this method is that the promotion is field-tested before going national, so avoiding the risk of both financial loss and promotional failure.

6. SET A CLEAR REWARD STRUCTURE

Apart from deciding what the prizes, awards, and extras are going to be, and whom they will be for, the usual reward structure today is for there to be one major prizewinner in competitions, with a good spread of runners-up, so that people feel that they have a good chance of being some kind of winner. (If the aim is to use the entrants' names and addresses for mailing purposes, then it must be made plain at the outset that this is the case.) When it comes to redeeming coupons, handling self-liquidating offers, and processing all the other awards being promoted, the promoter must be able to deliver what has been promised or make plain that there will be an alternative available. Nothing infuriates customers more than not receiving their reward, or not receiving it within the time stipulated.

7. DECIDE ON AN IMPLEMENTATION PLAN AND CHECK IT RIGOROUSLY

First of all, set out the plan for implementation, i.e. what is to be included. Check, once more, the idea behind the promotion, then the designs, artwork, and print. Carry out a proper search for all the other suppliers who may be called upon in running the scheme with you, and brief them thoroughly. Where necessary, draw up agreements with them and make sure they are fully integrated into your plans. Check budgets, handling houses, insurance, the legal position, delivery dates, factory and sales team support, trade co-operation, and the media (including public relations). Then, check everything again.

Implementation checklists will of course vary depending on the type of promotion being organized. For some, this may entail setting up tele-marketing and database marketing activities, door drops, roadshows, exhibitions, and sampling. Think about protection against copying, and any restrictions and conditions that might be imposed.

8. TAKE LEGAL ADVICE BEFORE RUNNING INTERNATIONAL PROMOTIONS

Not many national promotions can be run internationally. Although a similar theme might work, the detail will probably have to be amended to meet local laws. The pros and cons of working globally have already been highlighted, but it is advisable always to talk to a promotions lawyer who has practical international knowledge before attempting such a risky move.

9. EVALUATE THE SUCCESS OF YOUR PROMOTION

It might seem obvious that you should discover whether your promotion has been successful or not. But what are the benchmarks by which it will be judged? Three measures should form the basis of the evaluation – promotional response (from whichever source); sales figures from before, during, and after the event; and the total costs of running the promotion. Keep data and statistics for each event, and also comments made about them, so that a proper record is held for future reference.

10. CONDUCT A TOTAL REVIEW

Did the promotion work? How did the actual results stack up against the objectives set for the brand (e.g. market penetration, market share, budget, timings, etc.)? Would you do anything differently next time? Indeed, would you run a promotion at all next time? What could you have used the budget for that might have brought better results for the company (e.g. designing a new product)? Did the promotion actually make a profit contribution? Never shy away from harsh truths, and face up to reality.

CONCLUSION

If one follows the broad scope of these 10 steps then, apart from applying that spark of creativity, a more successful promotion should be within your grasp than otherwise would be the case. There is no doubt that sales promotion as a marketing tool allows the freest rein to creative minds to conceive schemes that can give enormous fun and pleasure to millions of folk who wish to take part. However, this free doing can be a double-edged sword and, in today's highly competitive and increasingly professional marketplace, great care has to be exercised by those who seek to use it to build a more profitable enterprise. This book on sales promotion can only take the reader or practitioner so far. The real results come from practice and experience. Good marketing is all about maximizing sales and profits, while reducing risks. Sales promotion plays a vital role in achieving these aims.

Frequently Asked Questions (FAQs)

Q1: What is the difference between competitions, free draws, instant wins, games, and lotteries?

A: Competitions offer prizes for the successful application of a certain level of skill (whether mental or physical) or judgement. Those who participate may be asked to pay to enter or make a purchase.

Free draws make prizes available by distribution of random chances. There is no requirement for any skill or judgement to be exercised and, accordingly, there is no requirement for any payment or purchase.

Instant wins offer prizes by distributing a set number of winning tickets. No skill or judgement is necessary, so entrants do not have to pay or make a purchase. Those who participate know instantly if they have won something.

Games are basically forms of free draw or instant win which, although they give the appearance of requiring skill, really rely on probability. Because no significant level of skill or judgement is required, no payment or purchase is necessary to enter. (Note: It does become confusing when you learn that people pay to enter games of chance such as bingo. They do, but these events are governed by the Gaming Act 1968 and a whole host of other regulations. The purpose of these regulations is to try to restrict the availability and (dubious) attraction of gambling, so that it can be taxed and controlled.)

Lotteries are the same as free draws except that entrants pay to participate. They are heavily regulated under the Lotteries and Amusements Act 1976.

See Chapter 8 for more details.

Q2: How can not-for-profit organizations benefit from sales promotion?

A: There is virtually no organization that cannot benefit from some form of sales promotion. Nowadays, many organizations such as charities and churches have ranges of merchandise that are sold for profit. Also, charities that rely on donations now offer free pens and other low-cost items to encourage people to give and to act as reminders. However, many charities currently link up with a commercial undertaking in a joint promotion having agreed how much the charity is to gain from the exercise. Care must be taken in deciding with whom to join up, so that both parties are equally satisfied with the results.

See Chapter 8 for more details.

Q3: What are the most popular prizes, and how many should there be in a prize structure?

A: Holidays, cars, houses, and cash, with holidays and cars top of the list as they are usually of a higher standard than those usually enjoyed by the entrants. As to the structure, the best system is to have one major prize and a goodly number of runner-up prizes.

See Chapters 7, 8, and 10 for more details.

Q4: Who can advise on a form of promotion that has no known precedent and may require legal advice?

A: Your first stop should be with the Institute of Sales Promotion, who may then suggest you contact the well-known specialist Philip Circus of Lawmark and his colleague Dr Richard Lawson. Their contact details may be found in Chapter 9.

Q5: Are there any moves to alter the way promotions are designed and operated as a result of the EU's involvement in marketing communications?

A: The EU seeks to harmonize consumer protection across Europe, but the sales promotion industry in the UK has a very strong code of practice, which is pledged to advocate legal, decent, honest, and truthful promotions. It is not thought that any promotional activity carried on in this country, and based on this code, should fall foul of any prospective directives from Brussels. However, it would be wise to keep abreast of any changes that may be mooted and later enacted.

See Chapters 5, 6, 9 and 10 for more details.

Q6: Will e-business bring about a major change in the way that promotions are organized and run?

A: It must be remembered that e-business is merely another form of communication and that the basic tenets of sales promotion will still apply, no matter which medium is employed. Having said that, those who think creatively enough about the opportunities that could be created by promoting on the Internet will inevitably bring to bear new and exciting ways of engaging their market via promotions specifically designed for this medium. However, like many ''new'' developments, the Internet will probably take its place in the promotional firmament, along with all the others that have served marketers and promoters so well for so long.

See Chapter 4 for more details.

Q7: How can I arrive at a sales promotion budget for my brand?

A: Don't try to spend what you think your competitors are spending. Their needs are totally different to yours. Don't spend what you spent last year and add a bit for inflation. And don't spend a fixed percentage of your brand's turnover. None of these methods will reflect on what you need to spend to achieve your goal or on what you can afford. So, work out what has to be done with the finance your company can afford and stick with it – otherwise you could bankrupt the business by going for unrealistic and unaffordable targets.

See Chapters 6 and 10 for more details.

Q8: How can my staff become more professionally qualified?

A: Contact the Institute of Sales Promotion, who arrange courses and examinations for those who wish to attain a professional standard. Their contact details may be found in Chapter 9.

Q9: Which promotion is right for my brand?

A: This is impossible to answer as every brand/product has its own promotional requirements. However, think of *offer*, *media*, and *image* and see which of the three dictates the other two. Check: What is the goal? Who is the target? What do we want to say (offer)? Where and by which medium should we say it (media)? How should we say it (image)? Create a shortlist and then spark the creative ideas! Never easy, especially when you have to concern yourself with the legal and financial niceties as well.

See Chapter 10 for more details.

Q10: What are the penalties for falling foul of the law regarding promotions?

A: Companies of all sizes fall foul of the laws covering promotions – some innocently, others flagrantly. The promoter will carry prime responsibility for all elements of a promotion, although service agents will share some elements. The local trading standards officer polices pricing and trading issues, while complaints can be made direct to the Office of Fair Trading, who have powers to impose sanctions and penalties on miscreants, along with the Advertising Standards Authority. Court cases are not unheard of in more serious areas of wrongdoing, and the ultimate punishment is imprisonment or a fine (or both) for the chief perpetrator. Possibly the worst that will be suffered by companies who innocently fall foul of some aspect of the promotional laws is the bad publicity generated by the media and by word of mouth.

See Chapter 6 for more details.

Index

Printed and bound in the UK by
CPI Antony Rowe, Eastbourne

Printed and bound by CPI Group (UK) Ltd, Croydon, CR0 4YY

13/04/2025